Paul Margueritte

L'avril

A Novel

Paul Margueritte

L'avril
A Novel

ISBN/EAN: 9783337028244

Printed in Europe, USA, Canada, Australia, Japan

Cover: Foto ©Thomas Meinert / pixelio.de

More available books at **www.hansebooks.com**

A Novel

TRANSLATED FROM THE FRENCH

OF

PAUL MARGUERITTE

BY

HELEN B. DOLE

———◆———

NEW YORK: 46 EAST 14TH STREET

THOMAS Y. CROWELL & COMPANY

BOSTON: 100 PURCHASE STREET

PRESS OF
Rockwell and Churchill
BOSTON

L'AVRIL.

I.

"Oh! this train, this train!" exclaimed Madame Rugles. "When shall we get there?"

Her restless feet were beating a march on the foot-warmer, now grown cold.

"Don't lean out so far, Jean," she said,

drawing back her son, a tall young man; but he, giving way to the exasperation which attacks the weak and nervous when they feel helpless, exclaimed in an irritated voice:

"It's a shame, a shame!"

Ever since they left Toulon the train had crawled along, making tiresome waits, whistling desperately in the darkness, continually threatening to stop in distress at the bottom of a grade. Something about the machinery had broken. Jean was on the point of rushing to the door again to question the master of the little station, in front of which they had been standing for a long quarter of an hour, when Madame Rugles seized his arm forcibly, but gently. Seeing him more vexed than herself made her become quite calm; moreover, she feared that he would only get into a useless and perhaps dangerous quarrel. Both turned towards a delicate figure stretched out on the seat.

"You are not getting too tired, are you, my poor darling?" asked the mother.

"You are not cold, are you, Minnie?" asked Jean.

The tenderness of their voices explained their impatience ; their anxiety was evidently on account of the young girl. She threw off the shawls which were wrapped about her and straightened up her slender form. Her face, in a tangle of yellow hair, seemed, in the light of the lamp above, singularly pale, with her gleaming hollow eyes, wonderful eyes, prominent and very near together, shining like orbs of greenish gold. A subtle fire, a soul keenly alive, animated her features with an inward glow like a porcelain night-light ; and she seemed equally flickering and restless, at the mercy of a breath of air which would extinguish this glow, or a touch which would break the fragile Saxony of which she seemed formed.

" Perhaps you will go to sleep," said the mother, deploring the unnecessary interruption of her rest, which she felt sure would be followed by restlessness and thoughts filled with the fear and mystery of night. Sleeping in the same room with her daughter, she almost always awoke whenever she did ; how many times she had caught the flash of anguish coming into those childish eyes, opening once more to the life of suffering, to the unknown of the present moment and of the future.

"I wish I could !..." and the young girl jumped to her feet, merely suggesting a modest line of life, which vanished as soon as it was traced beneath the falling folds of her skirt.

"What silly dreams one has ! They are so vague, so confused, so useless," she added, shaking her head to dispel the lingering vibrations of this thought.

Jean drew out his watch, tossed his head, pressed the indicator, put it back in his pocket, and said :

"Only think of it ! Two hours and a quarter behind time and three more stopping-places. Wretched train, go on !"

He suddenly closed the window. Minnie was coughing. Madame Rugles did not look at her but compressed her lips, folded her arms, and became rigid, as if she could not bear the cough which gave her a heartache.

"Bah ! we are no worse off here than anywhere else!" And Minnie looked about her with an air of doubt, and making up a face as though she suspected the exact propriety of this common *salon* for first-class passengers, where so many people were sitting, and which was impregnated with an equivocal odor of anonymous humanity, a suggestion of stale cigars added to the smell of varnish.

An association of ideas immediately aroused in her a feeling of homesickness, a longing for their dear little country house at Mortefontaine, and a dread of the furnished villa they expected to rent for the winter at Saint-Frégose. She was weakened, moreover, by the jarring of the express-train. The feeling of her helplessness, borne along by the irresistible speed of this brutal force, plunging through the dark country, through gloomy forests, over pale rivers, past the lighted stations, finally caused her so much distress that she threw her arms around her mother's neck and kissed her.

This spontaneous effusion seemed to say, plainer than words:

"Do not suffer for me, dearest mamma!"

Madame Rugles understood it, and so did Jean. These three people loved one another tenderly, and understood one another's thoughts. It often happened that one would speak the very words that the other was going to say ; this harmony was especially striking between the two young people, who were alike in every way. Jean looked at them, the mother holding Minnie's hands in her own, with a solemn air of protection ; Minnie taking refuge in her mother's arms, both in one of those communions of the soul which are silent, seem meaningless, and yet contain all the intensity of which human emotion is capable.

"Poor little sister!" he murmured to himself, full of adoring tenderness, which gave place to fears which, if not imaginary, at least he hoped were too lively not to be exaggerated. The winter spent in the sunshine would be an excellent thing ; the sea air would give strength to the delicate young girl. Instead of considering her case dangerous, had not their old friend, Doctor

Farus, seemed reassured by the resistance
her nervous system had offered to the
encroaching anæmia, the languor, brought
on in consequence of a first disappointment
in love?

" Poor little girl ! "

A fierce hatred hardened his heart against
all the Davenne family, against his uncle
Pierre, his aunt Lise, and especially against
his cousin Guy, whom he had loved like a
brother until now, and whom he detested
and despised since he had seen him yield,
without any apparent resistance, to his
father's tyranny ; for Monsieur Davenne had
pronounced an irrevocable sentence against
all possibility of a union between his son and
his niece, although he had allowed them to
grow up side by side without any mistrust,
even smiling on this affection which he now
discountenanced, since the death of his
brother-in-law had left the Rugleses half
ruined. Without doubt, he felt that the
difference was too great between them and
him, since he was an engineer who had
made a fortune abroad, had been chosen

deputy at the last election, and — who knows? might be minister to-morrow.

Jean thought over the scenes which had upset the family, tragic scenes in reality, although seeming foolish, and bordering on that frequently burlesque absurdity which pathetic circumstances assume when fine action and effective words are almost always depreciated by care for appearance, vain or selfish little prejudices, the unconscious and honest unreasonableness of phrases.

His aunt, usually sweet, now bitter and hostile, bristling like a fat hen; his uncle, puffed up with authority, red as a turkey; and Guy, with his long neck like a heron's, timid and silent, — these three people seemed to him like strangers, enemies, odious, without any real or possible relationship. To think that his mother had begged them to relent! His uncle Pierre had remained immovable, and to remove Guy to a safe distance he managed to have him chosen as a representative of the government at the Chicago Exposition.

Four months had passed since then, and Minnie, left without a ray of hope, had never

once opened her mouth to pronounce her
cousin's name. If she should die in consequence of this refusal! Hopeless misery!
What heartless brutes those Davennes are!
Oh! to become suddenly rich, to inherit
millions, and to throw the money in their
faces, crying:

"We will buy your Guy of you! Minnie
will pay for him and marry him!"

The train was now moving on, still at
an exasperatingly slow pace; and at the
end of this long journey, after the dull day
and the sleepless night, it seemed to the
Rugleses as if they would never reach their
destination. The rest they had taken while
breakfasting at Marseilles in the old seaport
had increased their weariness by filling their
brains with pictures of the noisy streets
crowded with passers-by and vehicles. The
cold meat on which they had dined in the
train was a burden to them; they yearned
for the unconventional comfort, the intimacy
of a home. But in the minds of Madame
Rugles and Jean, above all this little trifling
covetousness rose a cruel anxiety in regard

to Minnie, the fear that she might be taken
ill, that this excessive fatigue might aggra-
vate the slow fever she had every night; it
was this that filled their thoughts as they
looked at each other, while the invalid,
having returned to her corner, was looking

out into the darkness and trying to get a
glimpse of the sea near which they were
passing, and the salt odor of which they
could smell in the east wind, blowing in
gusts, full of electricity and rain.

"And this weather," murmured Madame
Rugles, in a tone of exaggerated despair,

which women put even into their most legit-
imate annoyances. "Even the weather is
against us!"

She added:

"Will there be even an omnibus at the
station? Everybody will be asleep at such
an hour. Where shall we find a hotel?"

Jean confirmed her fears:

"We shall not reach there until half-past
twelve or one o'clock!"

She grumbled, and could not refrain from
giving further expression to her irritation:

"I do not understand why we have heard
nothing from the Esslers. It was through
them that we were led to come to Saint-
Frégose, and when we decided at the last
moment and wrote to them we received no
reply!"

Jean shrugged his shoulders, probably for
want of an explanation. Silence ensued,
heavy with the need of sleep, tinged with
melancholy resulting from the dull, yellow
light in the railway carriage. Irrepressible
yawns, hardly concealed behind their hands,
their polite patience having come to an end,

stretched out the faces
of Jean and his mother
with an expression of
despair like Japanese
masques; Minnie felt the contagion; she
showed her white teeth and the rosy inte-

rior of her mouth, like a cat ready to bite, with a sudden feline and purely animal grace. It was as if something of her inmost femininity, of her sensual reality, was disclosed. Jean had a subtle intuition of it, and could not help following the contour of this beloved silhouette, the sloping shoulders, the curves of her youthful waist, her skirt falling over her hips and concealing the rest of her body; Minnie seemed charming to him, not only as a sister, but also as a young girl; he understood how exquisite and desirable she must appear in the eyes of other men, and this caused him almost jealous pain, because there was an indefinable element in his pure, respectful, and familiar tenderness for her. He was aware that it was something more than a fraternal charm which she exerted, it was the immemorial attraction of her sex; it was the flower and perfume of the eternal Eve which she carried about in her dress, and he could not help breathing and delighting in the sweetness of it.

The way in which he was gazing at her made the young girl feel that she was watched, as much as if he had really touched her; she turned around, and, moving quietly, dropped down by his side and leaned against his shoulder. This caressing contact broke the charm : he felt cold beside the undoubted insexuality of this body. Minnie was only his sister; the ideal phantom disappeared, and gave place to the materiality of a well-known, familiar being, dispossessed of the secret magic which adorned it with graceful carriage and charming dress. Affectionate, but unenthusiastic, he pressed the little hand gloved in soiled Swedish kid, while he noticed where her dress had been mended in a fold of the material ; the long, slender, childish foot, high in the instep, in a button boot, was to him nothing more than a foot.

Their mother watched them with fond and anxious eyes. She was once very beautiful : now her features were almost lost in the rubicund fulness of her face, but she had wonderful ashy-gray hair, and her kindly eyes and mouth gave her an air of matronly dignity. There was a slight awkwardness

about her **tall** figure, which is not **without**
its **charm in** people of unusual height, and
this made her sometimes undecided in her
bearing. However, **it** was easy to see that
she was really affectionate, self-sacrificing,
and very determined. She had suffered a
great deal during the life **of** her husband,
whom she adored, and who had abused her
indulgence ; and after his death, **two** years
before, she had been obliged to struggle
through perplexing difficulties, and to sell
the manufactory **he** superintended at Pu-
teaux.

Instead **of the** customary fortune, horses,
carriages, fine style of living, there was only a
modest competency, **a** fourth-story apartment
in Paris, a small summer-house in the **coun-**
try. She had proved herself so brave in all
this that **her** brother, the terrible uncle
Davenne, had admired her. He had disap-
proved of only **one** thing, that she had con-
sented to **take Jean** from the Henri IV.
school, **where, to** tell the truth, he had done
little **work, and put** him as a half-boarder in
the Gaussin institute. **There he took** the

first part of his degree, but had just been refused the second.

Without doubt, it would have been wiser to leave him to board all winter in Paris, but he had promised so faithfully to work at home that she had yielded in order not to separate him from his suffering sister; and he, knowing well the strength and the weakness of her maternal affection, was thinking it all over with a crafty and contented gratitude, beneath the generous, trusting gaze which she fixed on him : a dark look, which he felt was still full of vitality, although she seemed, in her whole being, worn out with the journey, older and more dejected this evening, with a smile telling of her despondency under the burden of hours of travel, and perhaps, too, of years of life.

How long would they have to wait, with their eyes full of sleep, which was gradually overpowering them?

Suddenly the name of the last station before Saint-Frégose sounded. They started to their feet, quickly strapped up their

shawls; Minnie put on her hat; Madame
Rugles looked for a missing glove. And
now they were almost surprised that it was
possible they were so near their journey's
end. Their eyes took a last look at the com-
partment which they would probably never
see again, and which had held something of
themselves.

" Saint-Frégose ! " cried the ringing voice
of a Provençal employé.

They were the only ones to leave the train
— stepping on a slippery platform reflecting
the light in melancholy patches; the trees
rustled in the middle of a square; walls with
closed shutters stretched out their funereal
bareness; here and there yawned plots of
ground bristling with fences. It was impossible to make out whether they were in a city
or a village; everything was black and indistinct — sheds or ruins smelling of wet clay,
mouldy plaster, and wood. The wind blew
through the empty streets; not a soul was to
be seen; a single ray of light glimmered from
a street lamp in the distance; it was dismal !

" Cover up your mouth well, Minnie !

But, dear me, what shall we do ! Monsieur, monsieur, if you please. Oh, dear ! We cannot sleep in the street ! "

This voice of distress, so innocent and almost comical, his mother's alarm, shocked Jean's childish self-love ; for he fancied, like other young people, that ironical eyes and ears were open to watch those whom he was with as well as himself. He replied aloud :

" But it is not so late. It will not be hard to find a hotel ! "

He said this purposely before the guard as he was giving him the tickets, with the air of a traveller who knows where he is going. In what direction it would have been very difficult for him to decide ; but a dwarf, whose head was in the middle of his body, and was covered with dirt to the top of his hump, arose before them as if by magic :

" Hôtel de Savoie ? All ready ! "

He took the wraps and the valise with authority, and walked on ahead, a real providence. To the timid questions of Madame Rugles, whose feminine sensitiveness had felt Jean's coldness, almost amount-

ing to rudeness, he replied with incomplete
sentences :

"The oldest hotel in the country; very
good, not dear ! Train late. Fell asleep in
the waiting-room ! Fortunately for you, or
you would have found nobody to meet you ! "

They followed him meekly, both reassured
and distrustful on account of his ragged
trousers. He stretched out his spider-like
legs, turning towards them, all awry, a flat-
nosed, roguish face, with a child's cap over
his forehead. They had passed under the
railway-bridge, leaving the roof of a little
market on their left, and crossed one or two
narrow streets, when he entered an alley
lighted by a lantern, and went in between
four elms forming a sort of grove, and con-
nected by a green lattice-work.

"There ! " And setting down the shawls
and valise he began to knock on the door
with all his might, calling out :

"Moussu Loustigarel ! "

Nobody answered, and he knocked again,
calling louder, till, tired of bruising his hand
to no purpose, he began to kick the panel

with his foot. This racket, together with the mean appearance of the house, more of an inn than hotel, rough cast with a dirty yellow, with atrocious green blinds, strangely dilapidated and dingy, made a painful impression on the two women, who timidly drew close to Jean. They thought they might have to stay in the street, and at the same time they were afraid to pass the night in this house. At last the hunchback shrieked for the twentieth time, detaching each syllable, and drawling it out immeasurably.

" Mou...ssu...Lous...ti... gaa... rrelll ! " A window opened on the first floor, and a sleepy, grumpy voice demanded if there was a fire.

A few moments later the door was unfastened and a man in trousers and shirt-sleeves, hairy as a faun and with a Madras handkerchief on his head, stepped back to let them enter. Seeing the ladies, he disappeared, muttering excuses, which Madame Rugles took for disagreeable words. Her first demand was for a fire in the rooms, and this won the consideration of the humpback for her.

He went on before them gravely, a candlestick
in his hand, up the staircase paved with red
tiles, along dubious passages where large
shoes trodden down at the heels stood in
pairs, ignorant of their ugly and almost ridiculous appearance. The key turned and
the Rugleses found themselves in a room with
two beds, communicating with a smaller
chamber, which was assigned to Jean.

The dwarf's deformity, as he placed the
matches on the table by the bed, seemed
even more forbidding in the light; and the
huge shadow that he cast against the white
beds and walls, as he went back and forth
between the two women, seemed almost a
violation of privacy in a room so vulgar
and common. They were obliged to toler-
ate his intrusive presence, because he was
piling up the wood and kindling fir cones,
the fragrant but pungent odor of which
affected Minnie's throat. She stood looking
steadily at the fireplace, watching the man
as he made up queer faces at the blaze like
a gnome, picking up the gleaming cones in
his fingers without burning them.

Finally he wished them good night and went out, leaving his cap on a chair; Jean noticed it and went to call him back, but he had disappeared. Madame Rugles in disgust seized the black rag like a great toad with the tongs, and put it out in the hall to associate with the impudent shoes; this was of no consequence in itself, and there was certainly nothing wrong about it, but it marked so expressively the difference of caste and the miserable inferiority of the slave, of the Caliban destined to hard, low service, that Jean wished that his mother had taken the tattered thing with her fingers and not placed it on the bare floor. This scruple haunted him with such force that he could not help going out to pick up the cap and put it at the head of the stairs in plain sight on a trunk.

When he came back Madame Rugles, raising her candlestick in the air, was inspecting the worm-eaten woodwork and dirty papering; she then examined the uneven mattresses, hollowed out in the middle, and looked to see if the sheets were clean.

"Well," she murmured, shaking her head, "a night is soon over. What are you thinking about?" she asked her daughter.

Minnie was standing still in the same place, looking into the fire, absorbed in her thoughts. She started suddenly, as though

wakened from a dream. Her face had assumed a singular expression.

"It is not gay," she said, "our arrival.
And what a place, mamma !... Oh, no, it is
not lively. Saint-Frégose is not at all lively."

She tried to smile, but her eyelashes
drooped, her voice choked, she shivered.
She said :

"I am cold."

Madame Rugles took her by the shoulders
and made her sit down by the fire. Kneeling
down, she began to take off her boots, as
though she were a child, then rubbing in her
hands the little cold feet in black stockings,
she held them out to the flames, replying, in
a tone of indescribable tenderness, to the
young girl's resistance :

"You must let me. I am going to undress you, my child."

II.

WHEN Jean awoke, the yellow dawn was shining in at the top of the blinds, the lower part of which still rested in bluish daylight. He jumped from his bed and opened the window.

In the fresh light, palm-trees extended along an avenue as far as a church that looked too new and too large. It was built in a strange Byzantine style of archi-tecture. It overlooked the sea, glimpses of which could be seen between the houses, and lofty mountains in the distance bordered the horizon. On every side there was a

contrast of dirty old hovels, out of all harmony with the new five-story houses beside
them, the whole scattered, built indiscrimi-
nately on plots of ground here and there,
and, in spite of the advertisements in the
newspapers, bearing decided evidence of the
winter watering-place, showy and empty, too
hastily grafted on to the village of fishermen,
which Saint-Frégose had been three years
before. Jean dressed quietly, for it seemed
to him as if they were still sleeping in the
next room, after a restless night, during
which he thought he had heard his mother
get up several times to cover up or care for
Minnie.

The door opened very softly, and Madame
Rugles, gliding in cautiously, said to him in
a low voice :

"Good morning, my dear Jean. Your
sister is not well. I am afraid she has bron-
chitis; she has been burning with fever all
. night; she is sleeping now. I gave her
some codeine to relieve the oppression. We
must try to find the Esslers, who can help us
select a house, and also a physician. But I

do not dare to leave Minnie all alone. See
how pale she is."

The frail young girl was sleeping, in the
dim light of the room. Her head was
raised with two pillows, her mother having
deprived herself of her own to give it to her.
Her difficult breathing moved the sheet over
her, and gave her face an expression of
effort and suffering which, together with the
deathly look of her closed eyes and her compressed lips, produced a strangely painful
effect. The circles around her eyes, her un-
evenly white complexion, the different shades
of her loose hair, the straw-color of which
was dark in some places, and paler like flax
in another, or in still others like strands of
old gold, — everything about her suggested
anæmic refining, a charm so perilous to a
human being. However, the exquisite round-
ness of her neck, the milky whiteness of the
flesh, showing above the ruffle of her night-
dress, were reassuring on account of their
healthful sweetness. The stupor of this en-
forced sleep was alarming, for throughout her
whole body, so oppressed and overpowered

by an invisible weight, it suggested the rigidity of another sleep, more profound and more terrible. It moved Jean to tears, and he shook with anger.

"Ah!" he murmured, "I would undertake to make her well! But that milksop of a Guy cannot love her seriously! and so !..."

His mother read in his eyes the opposition he would have advised his cousin to make, and which she feared he would some day offer to her, if he wished to marry against her wishes; she felt a secret dread:

"No, it would be wrong! Besides, if Minnie had married him, she might not have been happy."

But the thought that her child was suffering revived all her ill feeling; she seized Jean's wrist; her eyes sparkled:

"Never," she declared with determination, "never will I forgive my brother for being so hard-hearted. He has spoken against your father's memory, he has charged him with being the cause of our misfortunes. Oh! my child, get your degree, and then try to win back some of this miserable money, without which, in these days, you are nothing, and you have nothing ! If we were still rich, Minnie would be married, happy and well."

Despair made her beautiful, good old face look withered, and her voice trembled :

" But it is not possible that my child is dangerously ill ! You do not believe it, do you, my dearest ? "

" Mother ! " exclaimed Jean, with a foolish desire to throw his arms around her neck. " O mamma ! what are you thinking about? Is it possible ? "

" I do not really believe it," she said ; " oh, no ! It would be too terrible ; but you cannot blame me for having some fears. I am her mother, and she is not well, my poor Jean, she is not at all well !..."

" Come, mamma ! "

" Ah ! you are right ! " she continued, starting up and trying to control herself. " I beg your pardon, my dear, for troubling you so much."

He pressed her hand, which she had

dropped to her side, smiled at her consideration, and said :

"Come, the sunshine and sweet air of this
country are going to restore her ! If Saint-
Frégose does not seem lively, at least there
are not many invalids and no risk of contagion, and that is what Doctor Farus feared
above all things. It will come out all right,
you will see ! "

She sighed :

" But you must be hungry. Ring, and I
will order some chocolate ! "

A maid entered the room. She was strong
and large, with a rosy complexion and the
black eyes characteristic of the women of
Marseilles, with a free and easy way of dis-
playing the fulness of her throat and the
oscillating motion of her hips. She lighted
the fire and served the breakfast. Her ready,
winning smile displeased Madame Rugles,
but fascinated Jean. When she went out,
he followed her in his thoughts with the
indefinite secret longing of a young man, in
whom desire and regret for the unattainable,
kindled by a torturing timidity, are mingled

with complications of ridiculous imaginary
events, a voluptuous puerile air-castle. In
spite of this he had just been deeply agitated, but the sincere solicitude he felt as he
thought of Minnie did not prevent him from
buttering his bread carefully ; for life, at all
times, is made up of these incongruities,
penetrated by man's natural forgetfulness and
the familiar exigencies of the instincts. Jean
was hungry and found the chocolate refresh-
ing. It made him see the situation in a
better light.

Madame Rugles, who had scarcely tasted
anything, and had just placed in front of the
fire the little china pot, holding the rest of
the chocolate, so that Minnie might find her
breakfast warm when she awoke, put on her
hat and pinned it before the mirror.

" I leave your sister in your care, my
dear," she said. " The sooner we get into
the country, the sooner we shall be settled.
I shall try not to be gone long, and as to
selecting a house, I shall not decide on anything without you."

Having said this to gratify her son, who

expected in everything to be treated as the head of the family, she went to the bed, listened to Minnie's breathing for a moment, turned at the door to throw a fond, earnest kiss to Jean, and went out noiselessly.

" First the Esslers," she said to herself, and, going to the office of the hotel, she made inquiries of an old woman, as yellow as a quince and dressed like a housekeeper, whom she took to be the landlady. Madame Loustigarel closed her eyes reverentially, and informed her, with a mixture of condescension and servility, that Monsieur and Madame Essler — she pronounced the name with all the respect due to wealth — were living outside the town, in their *bbecauutiful* country seat in Valençor. If madame would like a carriage !...

"Ah ! I..." She stopped in surprise, she opened her eyes at the unexpected coincidence ; she pointed to the further end of the street, where, on a huge bay horse lifting up its feet as though it were dancing, a tall young man in cap and leggings, with a hunting-whip in his hand, was coming

into sight, followed by five or six dogs of
all sizes.

" Here comes Monsieur Essler's son, just
in time.   If you would like to speak to him,
I will call him.   Oh ! he knows my husband
well."

Madame Rugles did not care to do so ;
she had hardly seen her friend's son before,
and possibly she felt intimidated by his dis-
dainful, bored appearance.   Still it occurred
to her :

" If this young man pleased, he might let
Jean ride horseback ; for that is my dear
boy's highest ambition."

" Who is the best physician here ? " she
asked.

The landlady hesitated, doubtless afraid
of compromising herself.

" Monsieur Sarrazin is the oldest, and has
the best reputation.   He is rich.   He doesn't
trouble himself about everybody.   There
are some people who prefer a new-comer, —
Roger Bar, a young man.   You see him
constantly riding his bicycle on the roads.
He doesn't spare any pains."

"And where shall I go to find out about
hiring a house?"

"Near the wharf, at Carnibal's agency.
Is madame going to spend the winter here?
On account of the pretty young lady, I
suppose."

Madame Rugles cut the conversation
short and went out, going in the direction of
the church. "It is rather strange," she
said to herself; "this good woman has seen
no one but myself as yet, and is not
acquainted with my children, and still she
knows that Minnie is out of health. That
promises well."

She had no intention of entering the
church, and yet she went in. The new
stones exhaled a crude dampness, the oak
seats shone like mirrors, the windows looked
like brilliant Épinal pictures, the gold and
white altar glittered in a halo of glory, a
bluish light bathed the confessionals and
the side chapels; and all this was cold, vast,
empty; it bewildered the mind, and froze
all thought of prayer. Madame Rugles
sought in vain that warm atmosphere, full

of incense and magnetism, the mysterious
plenitude of which wraps you about and
puts your soul in communion with other
souls.

Nevertheless she prayed with wise fervor,
which was not so much a sudden aspiration
as an exalted lifting up of her thoughts.
Without asking for a miracle, she desired
from the bottom of her heart that Minnie
might be restored to health ; and if she did
not then feel as much trust and hope as she
might have wished, her maternal anguish
was, nevertheless, somewhat comforted.

When she went out, five public carriages
stood where there had not been a single one
a few moments before : they were evidently
waiting for her. Three coachmen raised
their hats, the others smiled, waving their
hands invitingly and holding open the door.
At a venture she took the first victoria,
asked the price, found it too dear, suspected
that she was being cheated, but, not daring
to make any objection, gave the Esslers's
address. The coachman bowed at hearing
this well-known name, touched his hat, and

cracking his whip, the two thin horses started off at a rattling pace.

They went along by the seashore ; a walk with a balustrade extended in a rotunda around a kiosk for music. Three large white hotels, with signs bearing gilded capital letters, showed here and there an open window in an occupied room ; all the others, screened with muslin curtains, remained closed.

Now and then they met a passer-by, some lady, who furtively took notice of the new face without seeming to do so. A large solitary establishment, new like the church and the hotels, surprised Madame Rugles : it stood behind an iron railing and a walk of serrate-leaved aloes and dwarf palms. Its façade with columns and Greek capitals had a theatrical, rococo appearance, and the two wings of the building were flanked with two galleries with glass roofs, bearing in flaming letters these words : "Club for Winter Visitors," on one ; on the other, "Inhalatorium ; " and still other letters were displayed on the front: "Hydrothérapie, Douches, Bains de Vapeurs."

"This, madame," the coachman felt it his duty to explain, "is not only casino and theatre, but also an establishment for invalids!"

"Dear me! How empty everything seems," she thought; "one would suppose that there were no occupants."

This impression was accentuated by the contrast of the scenery, so extensive and extraordinary, the bay making in to the land, and the distant mountains revealing in the direction of the nearest town — Argis, the spire of which could be seen — a melancholy landscape, delicately tinged with brown. Towards Cannes, on the contrary, the open sea stretched out, studded with rocky islands; under the clear sky it reflected the deep blue, dimpling away to the infinite, rolling on the shore gray waves heavy with seaweed. Without being too warm, the sun was mild and comfortable. The carriage turned to the left, between villas surrounded with gardens.

"Ah!" thought Madame Rugles, "so this is where the villas are!"

She looked at them with curiosity as she passed, noticing whether the blinds were open or closed, wondering about prices, delighted with the roses blooming on all the railings and mason-work, and climbing on all the walls.

"How good it will be for Minnie here, she loves flowers so much! There are a good many pines here, and their odor is said to be so beneficial! Wait, this is where the doctor lives."

A copper plate shining like gold, let into
the wall of a very large and beautiful villa,
bore this inscription :

DOCTOR SARRAZIN.
From 1 to 3. — English spoken.

Madame Rugles was almost tempted to
stop and ask the doctor to go to the hotel,
but she refrained, she knew not why, perhaps restrained by the insolent frown which
the coachman at the villa, engaged in rubbing
the harness, had just cast at her poor turnout.
She thought that in any case, living there, the
doctor would be at hand.

But a sight met her eyes which made her
laugh. She noticed in the distance, thanks
to her good eyes, a tiny cart, to which was
harnessed a donkey, about as large as a
goat. A lady had just taken her seat in it,
and a noisy band of children surrounded
her, three little girls and two boys, with
merry, rosy faces, the girls of fair complexion
burned scarlet in the sun, the boys dark and
curly-haired ; their free grace and their dress
denoted luxury and happy family life ; they

laughed because the little, obstinate, lazy donkey refused to budge. The mother, in

her seat, was laughing too, and they did not
stop when they saw the carriage approaching,
and a strange lady inside ; the pretty eyes
and happy laughter, on the contrary, seemed
to call Madame Rugles to witness Cadet's
obstinacy, for the tiny donkey was so named,
and the whole family were shouting : " Go
along, Cadet ! " while the boys, hanging on
his bit, were trying in vain to make him move
a single step.

The carriag had slackened its pace in
order not to run over them. The two women
looked at each other as they passed, and in
this short moment, not at once, but with a
slowly awaking intelligence giving rise to
reflection, a half-formed recognition passed
over their features, while they spontaneously
started towards each other, full of surprise and
yet afraid of being mistaken. The driver
whipped his horses, and Madame Rugles,
already at a distance, said to herself:

" Why, I know those eyes, I know the
color and expression of those eyes ; her face
is very familiar to me, but who can it be ? "

The proof that she was not mistaken was

that this lady had also looked at her as if she were going to speak to her ; perhaps she had recognized her at once. Less fortunate Madame Rugles tried to remember, and her inability to verify her impression tormented her keenly and painfully, as in dreams when an impossibility paralyzes you, so near are you to the attainment of your object. She thought over the past, recalled recent friendships, her social relations, even to people she felt no interest in ; and not one corresponded to that face, and especially to those eyes. How could she explain how it was that those eyes were so well known to her, so dear and familiar even in their violet sweetness, and that the face left her so undecided, baffled her inferences instead of determining them ?

" What is that lady's name ? "

The driver said :

" Madame Ferrier ; her husband is a retired colonel in the artillery. They have lived at Saint-Frégose for five years."

Madame Rugles's perplexity was still greater. Ferrier — the name suggested

nothing. And suddenly she exclaimed :
" Noémie !" so loud that the driver turned
round.

Noémie Crozette, a friend in the convent,
lost to sight for twenty years, never forgotten,
always thought of with regret, with the hope
of meeting her again at some turn in life,
some day. Why had she not recognized
her immediately by her sweet, kindly blue
eyes, so unusual? Doubtless because her
face, fuller and paler, did not correspond to
the thin, delicate features of the young girl
whom she remembered. It was she and no
one else ; settled down in a dark-blue dress,
her figure now grown so stout she seemed
short ; she had once been so tall and slender !
How mysterious the transformation of those
we have loved, whom we always think of as
they were when we saw them last, a painful,
melancholy reminder of the flight of time
and the approach of old age !

" Dear Noémie !" she sighed with a crazy
desire to order the driver to turn round, and
at the same time she felt glad to postpone
the certainty of the happy moment when she

would embrace her friend. A throng of
memories rushed into her mind, visions of
her youth, the interior of the large convent
at Aix, surrounded with peaceful gardens ;
and faces of other young girls, but none so
dear to her heart. How could she have let
so many years pass without knowing anything
about her? How could she have resigned
herself to that painful accustomedness, which
only shows us our absent friends lost in some
limbo, alive we hope, happy perhaps, ill or
dead, who knows? Ah ! how the life of
each day revolves like a millstone, wears out
the heart, crushes old affections ; and who
knows, after the burst of emotion which will
unite their hands and their lips, whether,
after so long a lapse of time, different in their
mode of living and their way of thinking, they
will find anything to say to each other, will
still be in sympathy, and will not experience
that frightful sterility of heart peculiar to
old friends who talk familiarly together and
exchange nothing but empty ideas?

"Dear Noémie ! yes, I believe it was she
who wrote last. She went to join her father

in America, and then remoteness, my marriage, selfishness, ah! surely the selfishness
of a young wife who loves her husband;
then the children, the cares, everything...!
No matter, I was wrong. As we advance in
years, we recognize the instability of the
best friendships; our change of fortune has
put more than one to the test!"

She sighed, and all her thoughts soared to
the pure, beautiful illusion of youthful affection, when as charming young girls, one
leaning upon the other, with their arms
around each other's waists like two sisters,
Noémie and herself looked at life with the
beautiful eyes of trust, and the smiles of
strong-willed artless maidens. Oh, their
dreams in those days, the hope, the liberty,
the winged power, the intimate attraction of
the grace with which they worked miracles,
— how long ago all this seemed...!

"Look, madame, from here you can see
the villas of Valençor, that beautiful place
with its gilded pinnacles is Monsieur Essler's
estate!"

Why was this recall to reality and the Esslers

painful to Madame Rugles? She had known
them only three years, since the time when
Monsieur Essler, contractor for footgear for
the army, superintended an enormous manufactory at Courbevoie. Since that time he
had sold his daughter and his business to a
son-in-law, retired and spent his winters in the
south. Monsieur Rugles had had pleasant
relations with him, and the two families became intimate. Since his death the relations
between his family and the Esslers had continued polite, though they were separated by
distance.

Without admitting it to herself, Madame
Rugles was counting on renewing their for-
mer intimacy, and innocently expected kind
attentions from them, and it never occurred
to her that there would be anything undig-
nified in this; they were very rich, but had
not she and her husband been rich also?

The comparatively comfortable manner of
living, free from immediate privation, which
she kept up sometimes made her forget she was
not still in possession of her past fortune, and
that she and her family were not still holding

a high position on account of their recent
prestige.

The carriage stopped in front of the
gate, rigorously closed, bristling with pointed
spikes, which were continued down to walls
cemented with pieces of broken glass.

As soon as the driver rang, a furious barking was set up. The shrill voice of the
Danish dogs and the yelping of the pugs were
mingled in a horrible discordant concert,
while the puffy-cheeked bull-dogs rushed out
growling.

The master's voice was heard above this
hubbub, and a tall gentleman, all red and
white, roughly rebuking the dogs, which
stopped barking except on the sly, appeared,
in morning-dress, wearing a cloth cap, with
pruning-shears in his hand. Monsieur Essler
did not recognize Madame Rugles at first,
and excused himself on account of his poor
eyesight. However, his eyes looked at her
with a strange, penetrating keenness. Those
eyes too round and too open were fixed and
critical, like those of very old cats, with a
cold hardness in their green, watery depths.

"Léontine is in," he said; "she will be charmed to see you."

Why did she fancy that an imperceptible uncertainty in the tone of his voice betrayed a lack of sincerity in his thoughts !

He took her through carefully raked paths, with borders as clean as an inlaid floor ; the plants had been washed till they could shine no more. The enormous aloes aroused her admiration, mingled with suggestion of fear, they seemed so formidable, stiff, and twisted, spreading out in all directions their fibrous serpentine knots all bearded with thorns.

" Joseph ! " called Monsieur Essler abruptly.

A gardener came rushing out from a clump of trees. Without saying a word Monsieur Essler pointed to a bit of broken glass, which made a sparkling blemish on the walk. The man stammered, almost falling down in his eagerness to remove the unusual fragment ; the master's silence gave the reproach a crushing effect.

" Léontine," said Monsieur Essler, who

seemed only now to remember Madame Rugles, "Léontine would have answered your letter, but she didn't find it until yesterday on her return from a little trip to Bordighière, where she has been with our cousins, the Flassmans."

He pronounced the name of the celebrated banker with a smile, and that smile was plainly meant for the Flassmans and no one else; it was the free-masonic and deferential greeting made by wealth to millions.

He showed Madame Rugles into the drawing-room, and Madame Essler came in almost immediately, in a loose morning-gown, wearing on her feet old slippers such as her friend surely would not have put on. Her dress was careless in every way, as is the case with so many rich women when they are in the country and have no motive for exerting themselves to look attractive. She kissed Madame Rugles.

"You see, my dear friend, I make no difference for you. I receive you in my dressing-gown."

This was friendly, almost too much so,

suggestive of too much freedom and condescension.

"So here you are at Saint-Frégose. Do
you expect to spend the winter here? I
hope that you are not seriously anxious about
your daughter's health. Doctor Sarrazin is
excellent in such cases. Have you consulted him already? What did he say?"

Madame Rugles, in surprise, told her
about their arrival in the night, and how
they had stopped at the Hôtel de Savoie.
Madame Essler was scandalized, and interrupted her with:

"But, my dear, who could have advised
you? It is an inn, it wants only com-
mercial travellers. People go to the Grand
Hôtel D'Angleterre or to the Palace Hotel.
You are not going to remain there, I suppose. It would be impossible as you are
situated."

"But I expected to hear from you, and
get the information I asked for on this very
point in my letter."

"Oh! my dear friend, your letter!..."

Monsieur Essler interposed, repeating the

version he had already given, and his wife
exclaimed eagerly :

"Yes, yes, not till I came back from
Bordighière — the Flassmans."

And she, too, smiled as he had done at
the thought of the banker....

Madame Rugles suspected that their urging
her to spend the winter at Saint-Frégose was
idle talk, and that perhaps, when they knew
her decision, their delay in replying was
owing to regret, fear of being intruded upon,
or lest they might have to render her some
service. In this case she was too proud to
come to trouble them very often. But was
this shade of less restrained familiarity, of
accentuated superiority, in Madame Essler's
tone, owing to the difference in their fortunes,
now so very disproportionate? She was not
kept long in doubt. Léontine, who was stout,
with short hands and feet, a face soft and
white, whose expression of sour sweetness
made one think of turned milk, said to her
in a low, confidential voice :

"Well ! my poor friend, how did you come
off, after all? You must have been terribly
annoyed."

A door closed quietly on Monsieur Essler, who disappeared. Madame Rugles drew herself up, and with an effort to seem calm and dignified reassured her friend, not without some sarcasm.

" Ah ! so much the better," said Madame Essler. " I believed that you were wholly ruined. I was told so — the Flassmans. Oh ! I am very glad ! "

Protestations, concealments, and insinuations led to detailed explanations about her poor friend's real position. As she went on with her story, the milk of Madame Essler's face grew more and more sour, as though she had expected something worse, assuming the ugliness peculiar to a person very much wrought up. While looking at her, alarmed by an uneasiness which she could not account for, but was painfully aware of, the truth all at once flashed across Madame Rugles's mind. She understood suddenly — and at this late day ! — that at the time of their mutual good-fortune, Léontine had always envied her, with that inexplicable jealousy that some women feel who begrudge

you your happiness, your good qualities, your
air of prodigal enjoyment.

She understood it, and this sudden intuition disclosed to her all the depth of her
meanness, how under cover of their pre-
tended friendship Léontine had always se-
cretly sneered at her, and how certainly she
had not felt sorry to learn of Monsieur Rugles's
death and the embarrassment in which he
had left his affairs. This was for her a painful mortification, for she had believed in the
Esslers's sympathy ; but if her self-love and
her natural goodness suffered from it, this
red-hot iron at least would cauterize her
heart. She felt above her rival, and regretted
only that she had ever believed in her,
and she did not feel in the least envious.
Oh ! surely not ! to see her triumph in her
turn, through the stupid, vain, and tyrannical
supremacy of money. Now she was oppressed by their house and their garden, she
needed fresh air so much. As soon as she
could she rose to go. Joyful barking was
heard, and when they went out on the steps,
Essler's son, returned from his ride, was dis-

mounting from his horse, in the midst of his
hounds.

" François, Madame Rugles."

He bowed, with Britannic coldness. Seen
near, his complexion looked yellow and
shrivelled, furrowed with fine wrinkles, the
mask of an old man of the world, bored to
death in the country, and finding no refresh-
ment in its verdure.

Monsieur Essler appeared with a bouquet
of tea-roses, which he had just gathered
" himself," and which he presented to Madame Rugles. She was consulting " Léontine "
about the selection of a villa, and stopped
to thank him.

" But," he quickly suggested, " we have
one to let, a very large house, with stable,
carriage-house, billiard-hall, and bath-rooms,
and perfectly sheltered, three kilometers and
a half from the town. Four thousand for
the season, that is the price to a friend ! "

" Oh ! " she objected in embarrassment ;
" the distance... "

He replied victoriously : " Pshaw ! with a
carriage ! "

"But, my dear, *they* have no carriage, and besides it is too large, much too large," said Madame Essler, in a tone meant to imply "much too dear."

Their good-bys, accompanied by the low growling of the dogs, were constrained ; and when the sharp, pointed gate closed behind her, and she had smiled at the Esslers for the last time, shut in like prisoners of their scornful, forbidding wealth, Madame Rugles felt truly comforted in being carried away at a rapid rate into the coolness of a ravine abounding with rock-roses, lentisks, and rose-mary. She then noticed that Monsieur Essler's politeness had cost him little, for the rose-buds forming the bouquet were worm-eaten, yellow, and faded. This was more revolting to her than all the rest, this more than all offended her essentially feminine sense of shame ; the tears came to her eyes. Ah ! friends !... And in her exaggerated distrust and suspicious ill-feeling, she hoped, against all probability, that it was not Noémie Crozette whom she had recently caught sight of, surrounded with her beautiful children, in the

little donkey-cart. Would even she, Noémie, recognize her? Would she give her a
correct and humiliating reception, like the
Esslers? Two such disappointments in one
morning would be too much !

At the mere thought of it, she was going
to ask the driver if there wasn't some other
way, if it was necessary to pass the Ferriers's
house.

But already, at a turn in the road, she
saw the children in the street, as she had
done before, but without Cadet. Had they
been stationed there to watch for her? She
saw them run off, go into the house, call
some one, come out again, and look at her
with smiles and curiosity. Madame Ferrier
came out immediately after, and they all
barred the way, their eyes sparkling with the
expectation of something new, anticipated,
hoped for ! Madame Rugles's heart, deeply
touched, almost stopped beating.

"Stop ! "

She was already jumping out, and her
friend was holding out her hands to assist
her :

"Henriette ! What a delightful surprise ! "
And Madame Rugles kissed her affectionately on her kind, honest cheeks, stammer-
ing :

"Ah ! Noémie, my dear friend ! "

III.

After five weeks Minnie's cough disappeared, she felt the reviving benefit of a winter of sunshine in this bright country. It seemed delightful in comparison with the plain of Mortefontaine, touched by the first frosts, strewn with dry leaves along the road, or compared with the muddy streets and icy fogs of Paris.

At first this sudden change of air had stunned her, intoxicated her, and they almost. feared that the depressing languor

which was weakening her might become a
sort of waking, morbid sleep, an open-eyed
torpor, prostrating her, leaving her without
energy, almost without breath, in the large
cane reclining-chair, placed for her where
the sunlight and shade intermingled, before
the steps of the villa in the shelter of a group
of mimosas.

Gradually, however, a feeble strength
came back to her; if she still kept to her
repugnance for roast beef and rare mutton,
she no longer refused the consommés of
meat juice which her mother brought to her.
She was getting over the instinctive dislike
for Saint-Frégose which their unpleasant
arrival had occasioned, and this was a still
better symptom; she was not yet accustomed
to the strangeness of this new home, to the
unfamiliar character of the walls, and the
strange furniture, deprived of all personality
from having been rented to every chance
comer; but she was less disturbed by it
all, and was resigning herself to it with a
semi-indifference, mingled, it is true, with a
great insensibility to things; for Minnie, like

all young people made helpless by illness,
believed that she was sicker than she was,
so that everything looked dark to her.

But her firm power of resistance and live
vigor were smouldering under this dis-
couragement of soul and body, and it was a
gratifying sign to Madame Rugles, watching
her behind the closed blinds in the drawing-
room, to see her from time to time smell of
a bunch of pinks which had just been sent
to her by their neighbors, the Ferriers, and
upturning her delicate face, smile at the
purity of the soft, blue sky, move her eyes
to follow the flight of some bird, or direct
them to a little black cat given to her by
Madame Loustigarel. She watched it with
interest and amusement as it capered, put
up its back, crept along, and made sudden
leaps like an arrow shot from a bow. She
had named him Pierrot, and at that very
instant she was laughing heartily, raising herself on one elbow, and admiring the silly,
little, live black clown, the disorderly play of
which finally ended in such lazy sleep in her
lap.

Madame Rugles sighed and left her post of
observation to give orders to the maids ; and
Minnie, tired of looking at **the cat,** — for
everything very quickly wearied her, — took
a book lying near her on a chair, and tried
to read. But her hands soon dropped under
the heavy weight, and her soothing and lull-
ing thoughts carried her away to dreamland.
She floated in a semi-consciousness of herself
and the scenery about her ; she noticed the
gentle slope **of the** garden down to the rail-
road and beyond, undulating, sombre verd-
ure, which, in her melancholy state of mind,
she compared to the verdure of a cemetery,
and which disappeared on the road following
the shore, where the open sea stretched out
its **milky** azure, like mother-of-pearl, as
glassy as a mirror and undulating with ellip-
tical ripples.

Through this panorama of light which
spread before her eyes, she was also looking
at herself, as in the transparence of a glass
without quicksilver, and **to** see herself, to
feel herself live and think, was **a** sweet,
strange suffering, **now** confused, and now

acute, sometimes reduced to the slender
thread of a fixed idea, oftener melted and
bathed in the immensity of the things of
which she formed a part.

Was she dreaming of the love, the unacknowledged hope of which she was so
unjustly suffering for, the short idyl ending in
a commonplace drama? Of what could she
be dreaming, if not of that, or of the sad,
ruminating thoughts of her illness? But she
thought of this love and Guy Davenne as
something and somebody very far off, out of
sight. Oh! this had not come about without
a battle, periods of agony, a discouraging struggle in a soul in love for the first time, clinging
to possibility, probability, even absurdity.

But having been obliged to yield, and —
what seemed especially painful — having
seen the man who ought to have defended
her, conquered her, and carried her away by
main force yield also, she had fallen from
such a height that she felt nothing but wonder
that she was still alive, as one feels in a
dream, where every limb has been broken in
falling to the bottom of an abyss.

Footsteps behind her sounded on the gravel walk in the garden. She was too weak and too deeply buried in prostration to turn around. Two little hands were sud-

denly laid over her eyes, placing her in a rosy darkness not without its charm ; these child-ish hands were cool and sweet. Whoever it was did not speak, for fear of being recog-nized by the voice.

"It is Lucien !" said Minnie.

There was a ripple of laughter. It was Colette, the oldest of the Ferrier children, and not Lucien; she had named him because she liked him better than his brother Jacques. But she was already very fond of Colette, and returned her kiss.

"Perhaps you were asleep," said the pretty young girl, who at fifteen years had all the charming, thoughtless grace of a young child, "and I waked you up?"

Minnie looked at the small face, her fresh eyes, fair, braided hair, her dress which did not reach the ground, but came just to the top of her boots; she envied this spring flower, this gay, innocent creature, so ignorant of life.

"You did not waken me," she said.

Colette exclaimed:

"Oh! what a pretty bracelet you have! When I am eighteen, papa has promised me a gold bracelet. I wish it might be like yours. I think it shows very good taste."

"My father also gave it to me," said Minnie, "for my birthday, the year he was ill...."

She did not add — "and died;" but Colette understood, and was sorry that she had thoughtlessly recalled this sad memory. So she changed the conversation and announced :

" I came to tell you that Lucien is going to take you out with Cadet, and as Jacques has been punished because he didn't know his lessons, I am going with you in his place to the Inhalator.... I cannot pronounce that name...to the establishment for ozone."

" But Lucien will come to breakfast just the same, will he not? "

" To breakfast, yes. Papa didn't wish him to, but your brother interceded for him, and mamma too. Your brother is very nice, and he looks like my big brother Raymond. No one at home thinks so, but when you meet Raymond, you must tell me if you do not think I am right. When I say that he looks like him, I mean especially that he reminds me of him, because their features are not the same, nor the color of their hair. I hope you will be pleased with Raymond, because I love him so much, he is so wise, so good ; and although rather serious, people

always feel immediately at ease with him,
they feel light-hearted and content with life.
There are some people, on the contrary, to
whom you feel an aversion at first sight.
Doctor Sarrazin, for example, is one of such.
I do not know why, but I wouldn't have him
sound my lungs for anything in the world.
Monsieur Bar is quite different. And yet!
Don't you find it disagreeable to have your
lungs sounded?"

But she remembered that she was remind-
ing Minnie of the state of her health, which
was not pleasing to her, and the feeling of
regret that she had seemed so indiscreet put
an end to her prattle. However, she added
after a moment's silence :

" But you are feeling well, are you not?
You look so well this morning. Wait, you
must let me kiss you again ! " There was
a sound of two honest kisses. " How glad I
am that our mammas found each other once
more ! You have no idea how delighted
mine is; she was quite overcome, and I
really believe that she had a good cry in her
room after she saw your mother. Papa too

is very much pleased, and he likes you all very much."

"But," said Minnie, "your parents are so good! If it were not for them, I believe we should all die of dulness here at Saint-Frégose. Your mother helped us select our house, one of the prettiest in the place, and so near to yours. We have to thank your father for getting it at a much cheaper rent than the Carnibal agency asked at first. You recommended your physician, Doctor Bar, to us. Mamma would have found it very difficult to get maids, and would have been imposed upon by the tradespeople; and a hundred little things which seem nothing in themselves and yet are very important in a household. Then again your father is so kind as to make Jean work, and every morning has him review his mathematics. Thanks to you, we have met some charming people, the Misses Hawkins, Madame d'Anfresse, the Silleroys, all the cream of Saint-Frégose society!" She laughed gayly as she said this. "Mamma too feels grateful, she is very happy, I assure you.... And so am

I ! " she added, taking Colette's hands ; and Colette kissed her again, saying :

"Yes, it is all very good, and you will see the fine walks we shall take in the spring. Did you know the Hawkinses are going to have a tennis-court in their park? It is very amusing. I hope you will play."

She changed her tone, saying :

"The only thing lacking is Raymond. How I wish he were here !"

This older brother, as well as the three sisters, Colette, Jeanne, and Andrée, were Noémie Crozette's children by a first marriage with Monsieur Jermyn, while Lucien and Jacques were children by a second marriage with Monsieur Ferrier. This brother was sailing in his little yacht, the "Aventure," along the Italian coast between Genoa and Mentone. Monsieur Jermyn, an American millionaire, had left his children a large fortune and his widow a dower, which would have enabled them to surround themselves with all the splendor of luxury, but Madame Ferrier, through delicacy towards her husband and her children of the second edition, who were less privileged in spite of the colonel's **fine** personal fortune, had the **good sense to** live with extreme simplicity, **the** economy of which was compensated **by** extreme liberality towards the poor, and active coöperation with beneficent works.

The hospital for old men at Saint-Frégose was a notable example of her work. She had built **it** and established the Augustine sisters there, from the mother-house at Clermont. But she **never** spoke of these things, **having the** modesty **of** goodness as well as **the** modesty **of** wealth.

"Ah! there come Lucien and Cadet," said Colette, offering her forehead to **be** kissed, and saying **a** merry "Good morning, madame!" **to** Madame Rugles, who was bringing her daughter's hat and wrap.

"Good morning, my dear child. You will take good care of Minnie; I intrust her to you, and to you, Monsieur Lucien, and to Cadet also. Baptistine!" she called.

The little Provençal maid had guessed why she was called, and was already hurrying **along,** holding between her fingers two large

lumps of sugar, which the young Lucien,
looking like an intelligent little brown crick-
et, seized with an air of importance to offer
in the palm of his hand to Cadet. The donkey crunched the two lumps, moving his lips
as if asking for more, and waving his long
ears back and forth in a very amusing way.
Then Minnie climbed on to the seat and took
the reins, pleased to drive, and becoming a
child again at play.

Cadet went fast, but not faster than Colette, who walked with a free, lively step,
with a look of pride and happiness in her
little white face. Lucien ran almost as fast.

All along the way, as far as the road by the
seashore, there was a stretch of gardens and
nurseries, where white, pink, red, and yellow
roses bloomed on sections of walls, in a
tangle on the fences, and whole fields were
filled with their fragrant harvest. As they
passed by, Lucien occasionally picked one of
the roses, and the two young girls would
scold him for doing so. It was to offer to
Minnie, and then Colette would be silent.
But Minnie would declare seriously :

"The next time I shall refuse it."

She took it, however, welcoming the child's affection, glad that he loved her, and proved it to her in his own fashion. Besides, did she not enjoy decorating herself with this stolen flower, the small pleasure of forbidden fruit?

They passed by the balustraded walk, the kiosk for music, the creamy blue sea, where the blazing sunlight danced. In front of the great hotels of dazzling stucco, omnibuses, their new varnish shining with liquid splendor, were standing or starting away at a great rate, always empty, the fine-liveried coachman full of hope, destined to meet with disappointment every time, and cracking his whip in the empty air. The *Inhalatorium*, all lighted up, its glass windows all ablaze, flanking the pasteboard palace of the Casino, stood out in the clear air. Cadet, after the third day, having stopped of his own accord in front of the door, stretched out his legs, and stood stock-still.

Minnie got out of the carriage.

The glass-covered gallery was carpeted

with mats, decorated with large Vallauris
pots, in shades of turquoise, amethyst, and
garnet, in which were growing yuccas re-
sembling bundles of swords, wide-spreading
palms, and plants like enormous hairy cater-
pillars. As soon as Minnie entered this she
felt giddy, as one does when breathing into
the nostrils the air of a steamboat saloon.
The electricity supplied by powerful bat-
teries, and absorbing the pure oxygen, exhaled a nauseous odor, made still more disagreeable by a keen pungency like that of
sulphur matches, making one cough.

Minnie never went in without a feeling of
timidity, for she had that diffidence peculiar
to people who are suffering, and to whom
treatment in common with others is painful ;
she dreaded to have the eyes of three or four
invalids, whose faces were not yet familiar to
her, turned towards her, from above the row
of mouths of inhaling tubes. So, for the first
few weeks, she would not have dared to come
if Madame Rugles had not accompanied her,
and, sitting near the ozone room, had not
watched her, and encouraged her with smiles

and cheering looks to inhale the invigorating
gas. This morning, however, she did not
miss her mother, who was kept at home,
making preparations for a breakfast to the
Ferriers. She even went into the hall quite
bravely.

Doctor Bar quickly came to meet her,
greeting her with easy familiarity, such as his
position allowed, a freedom in which she had
noticed from the first a very marked defer-
ence and sympathy.

" Will you be so kind as to take your place
there, mademoiselle? Please take long,
slow, steady breaths...."

This customary sentence he repeated a
dozen times at every session. Only when he
addressed it to the others he did not appeal
to their kindness, but assumed an impersonal
tone, the authority of which Minnie felt would
have offended her, if he had been speaking to
her. She noticed also the eagerness with which
Eugène, the waiter, with his towel under his
arm, brought her a little seat or a cushion for
her back. She was sensible to these attentions ; they flattered her, appeased somewhat

the almost hostile ill-humor she felt in having to submit, without being able to object, to the beneficent tyranny of the doctor and his treatment.

She seated herself in the chair which Doctor Bar offered her, before the long, black, wooden panel, the singular shape of which concealed the working of the ozone tubes. She leaned her elbows on the edge of the wide black table, between the little partitions separating the patients; in front of her rose a high, straight box, perforated in the centre by a nickel-bordered opening, like those through which you look at the views in a diorama. The doctor had just fastened to the mouth of it a nickel shell, the wide opening of which spread the gas over a larger surface as it issued and mingled with the air. Minnie drew near to this conch and breathed in the mysterious air coming out of it in a steady stream, while a roaring like water escaping from the faucets in a bath-room was heard, interrupted at regular intervals by a metallic clicking.

"Take deep, gentle breaths," said the physician.

She felt him behind her, watching her inhale the gas; his mere presence made her nervous, almost paralyzed her. When he passed on behind another person's seat, she was relieved. It was not because the young man displeased her. She had heard him so highly praised by the Ferriers, not only for his worth as a practitioner, but for his merit and goodness as a man, that she felt deeply interested in him; his perfect manners, his reserved and yet friendly bearing, the contemplative beauty in the expression of his rather heavy features, with deep black eyes and long fine beard, the whiteness of his carefully tended hands, his irreproachable black dress, all made a favorable impression upon her.

She remembered his first visit, when they had called him to the Villa des Cistes, the delicacy with which he had sounded her lungs; everything about him, his questions, looks, smiles, made her anxious to believe what he said, inspired her with that unreasoning confidence, a hint of which is the strongest force, the most efficacious means physicians have over their patients. When he gave his opinion about her health, she did not feel that it was all a "professional lie," as she was impressed by other men, old Doctor Farus, for example. At least towards her he showed nothing of that air of false confidence, the tone of assurance, the ready scribbling of prescriptions, and lastly the appearance of gentle quackery, which the profession perhaps demands after all. Had he been too decided, too reassuring, she would not have believed in him ; she would have been discouraged at the outset, and felt that it was useless to try his remedies, although declared unfailing.

The caution which he showed, on the contrary, when he first visited her, his slowness to pronounce a decided opinion, seemed to her a guarantee of honesty and discreet sincerity. Knowing very well that he would probably not tell her the "whole truth," since his colleagues believe it is their duty to disguise it when it is unkind, she per-

suaded herself that he would not lie like
the others, and that through what he ac-
knowledged or what he kept to himself, she
would know how to read or make out the
truth.

Declaring herself thus favorably disposed
towards her physician removed a great
weight from Minnie's mind ; accustomed as
she was to their old doctor, she felt afraid
of the voice and face of strangers, and especially of their strange eyes, sounding her
weakness and taking cognizance of her wasted
form. Nothing had shocked her modesty
more beforehand, and nothing seemed more
agreeable and more quietly comforting than
to find herself reassured.

He came to say :

" Would you like to rest, mademoiselle ? "

" I should be glad to do so. I feel dizzy."

He offered her his arm to conduct her to
the sunny conservatory, pushed a wicker chair
near a willow table, at which Colette, with
her hands spread out on the margin of an
album, was looking at some Italian views
while waiting.

"I feel as if I were intoxicated," Minnie replied to the young girl's friendly smile.

"So much the better," said Doctor Bar; "it is the ozone taking effect and working beneficially; you would better finish your treatment in the second room, where the

current is not so strong. Rest while you
are waiting."

He went to tell the other invalids to stop
inhaling and to take a rest also. She saw
them scatter in the conservatory, too few in
number for the empty grandeur of the hall:
a young woman the color of wax, an old
woman shaking with a hard, racking cough,
and walking along with the assistance of an
Augustine sister, a round-shouldered young
boy, with dull complexion and a face wrinkled
like the skin of a gray lizard, a tall, thin
gentleman, whose small yellow head looked
like a lemon.

In different stages of consumption, but
very much afflicted, they looked at the sea
or the green plants with indifference, somewhat intently, with eyes in which the fixed
idea of their malady separated them from
the outside world. With all this, they
did not wish to seem ill; at least such
was the case with the tall gentleman, who
whistled a short tune between two attacks
of hoarse coughing. Minnie had noticed
that they did not speak or bow to one

another when they came in nor when they went away, each seeming to take no interest in any one but himself, and pursuing a solitary treatment.

Now she understood, as she watched them, how imaginary had been her fear of ever becoming as ill as they were, even much less so. Instead of yielding to the dizziness as she had done at first, she repulsed the idea of ever coming to resemble them. It was enough to find herself in their presence to make her feel better, lighter-hearted, and to be hungry and thirsty to live. She only wondered why, in spite of the doctor's reassuring explanations, she was obliged to follow the same treatment, why she breathed the same agent of vital restoration, this ozone, which she knew, however, from hearing it repeated, acted as a modifier of the blood corpuscles, as a tonic, and that to this, after a week, she owed the return of her appetite, and sleep free from fever and nightmare.

Doctor Bar approached her; she met his penetrating, keen, calm eyes, which he directed towards her, and they encouraged

her more than all the assurances and promises
that he could make.

"Will you go into the next room? Ten
minutes will be enough."

And an indefinable expression in his voice
gave her confidence. An invincible instinct
made her feel that he would have looked at
her differently, that he would have spoken
to her differently, if she were threatened like
the other patients. There certainly would
not have been such a gentle warmth in his
eyes, that little smiling crease in the corners
of his mouth, and his whole personality as a
healer would not have exhaled that magnetic
fluid of hope, the influence of which she had
felt.

She smiled, and a rosy tinge of health, a
flame as of new life, the first for many weeks,
animated her features for a moment. With
a bow he opened the door for her; she
murmured:

"Thank you, doctor," noticing that he
too smiled a friendly, almost paternal smile.

84

IV.

Slightly weary, with an expression of
becoming melancholy on her face, and glad to
reach home, Madame Ferrier was pushing
open the garden gate on her return from a visit
she had been paying to Madame Lartigues,
the mayor's wife, when she saw her husband
coming towards her; while waiting for her,
he had been walking up and down a path

bordered with Bengal rose-bushes half bare
of leaves.

She smiled at him.

Scarcely at all gray, quick and vigorous, he preserved a military robustness, was
still very erect.　He wore a red rosette fastened to his white flannel jacket.　As he
approached her he closed a little volume
of Tacitus he was reading in Latin, for his
taste for the exact sciences was united with
a literary fondness for Roman antiquity, and
he employed his leisure moments in reading,
teaching his children, making experiments
in chemistry in a laboratory of his own;
but all this did not prevent him from
taking long walks or rides on his tricycle for
the sake of his health.

They looked each other full in the face
with the loyal eyes of old married people,
whose union late in life had given them
fresh affection and that second youth which
is made up of what is left from the first, and
which owed much to mutual self-regard, to
careful consideration for each other, and
thoughtful care without too much display

of affection nor too much familiarity, and
also to their dignified behavior before children already grown.

"How beautiful you look, madame!" he
said, greeting her half in earnest, half in
fun. "That dress is wonderfully becoming!"

"Don't laugh at me, Henri," she said, giv-

ing him an affectionate pat on the hand.
"You know that formal calls are very weari-
some to me, and I only make them when I
am obliged to do so."

"I had no thought of laughing at you, my
dear, when I said that your dress suited you
very well. That delicate heliotrope harmo-
nizes charmingly with your complexion."

"That is the color for old women," she
replied with a smile of pleasing melancholy,
and in a friendly way she removed a pine
needle which had fastened itself to his sleeve.
Looking at her steadily and with a hearty
smile, he asked :

"What would you say if I should tell you
a piece of good news?"

She read it in his eyes and exclaimed :

"You have heard from Raymond?"

She continued with a smile :

"Don't you think, Henri, that I ought to
be jealous, if he has written to you and not
to me?" But she hastened to add, pressing
her husband's arm : "No, no, Raymond
ought to love you as if you were his father.
It is only just towards you, for you treat him

as a son! He has written, he is well; does he speak of coming home?"

The continued absences of her oldest son were the source of her only anxiety, her only trouble in the peaceful happiness, in the calm, smooth haven where her life was passed. She ought to have been resigned to it, as Raymond's health depended on it.

Possessing a brilliant mind, when he left the Polytechnic school, after passing his examinations successfully, he fell a victim to overwork, a prey to typhoid fever, and in order to recover from the nervous exhaustion in which it had left him, the doctors had ordered him to give up all work, and recommended that this over-excitement of the brain should be followed by a purely animal life, given up to physical exercise.

Compelled to give up a career of hard work, fortunately rich enough not to be obliged to follow a profession, Raymond for six years had been travelling extensively, spending two winters in Cairo, going to Constantinople, to Tahiti, to the Cape, and to Japan. The long voyages had restored his health and

given him strength ; the vast, beautiful land-
scapes, without wearying him, had filled his
eyes with moving splendors, and his soul with
deep impressions. Two years before he had
realized his great desire to own a little yacht,
and with the help of his step-father he had
bought a fine sailer, the crew of which num-
bered two trusty sailors and a cabin-boy.
This yacht had belonged to the celebrated
painter Maurepas, and after his death it was
out of commission in the harbor of Antibes ;
the heirs, tired of waiting for a purchaser,
had parted with it at a very low price. Raymond, overcoming his mother's opposition,
lived on the yacht, happy in cruising along
the coast, fishing in the little gulfs, dancing
on the short waves, watching the sea change
its dress, and reflect the interrupted splendor of the sunlight or the pale track of the
moon. On land he hunted, climbed mountains ; but a feeling of homesickness always
brought him back to the water.

His sunburned face, his broad shoulders,
his arms swollen with strong muscles, all
testified to the marvellous cure, the benefit

gained by this life in the sunshine, wind, and
salt air ; and since he was prudent and delib-
erate, and ran no useless risks on squally days,
his mother had made up her mind not to
see him except now and then, not to follow
him except by the short bulletins about his
health, which he sent as often as possible,
whenever they touched land. More than
once, leaving the boat in the care of old Pilou,
his mate, he had taken the train and reached
home unexpectedly.

The mere thought of the possibility of
seeing him appear suddenly kept Madame
Ferrier on the watch, prevented her from
becoming over-anxious. Nevertheless she
hoped that Raymond would make a good and
happy marriage which would keep him on
land. She did not even desire a large fortune,
since he was rich enough for two. But he was
difficult to charm, or rather shy and timid ;
the healthful way in which he spent his life
left no room for dreams of love, and, without
admitting it, he clung to his independence, to
his life in the open air, to the freedom of the
sea. All this anxious care was expressed in

the eager, pressing question addressed by
Madame Ferrier to her husband, who replied :

"Yes, he is well, he is very well, and speaks
of coming home soon, very soon indeed." As
he said this, his eyes and his smile expressed
a special kindness, accentuated by a delicate
mischievousness.

"Henri, you are telling me this to pre-
pare my mind. Raymond is coming, isn't
he? Tell me quickly when, my dear, —
to-morrow ! to-day? Don't make me faint.
These emotions make me ill as well as
happy. Show me his letter, I beg you."

"Raymond is coming this evening, since
you are so impatient. He has left his boat
at Genoa, he will come by the express in
time for dinner, and here is the telegram."

Madame Ferrier seized the paper, flushed,
and became young again for the moment.

"You must allow me to see about having
his room made ready for him immediately.
What a pleasure it will be to see him again !
Why is it that the probability of his going
away again as suddenly as he comes always
spoils my delight?"

And she sighed, adding :

" Oh, how unfortunate it is that " —

She interrupted herself to say :

" Let us invite the Rugleses for to-morrow, will you? I am sure Raymond would like them, shy as he is. You have no objections ? "

" Quite otherwise ; I like Madame Rugles and her children very much," replied Monsieur Ferrier; " the son has good qualities, and something can be made of him ; as to the young girl, she is charming."

" Is she not? " she asked eagerly. " She is naturally lady-like, pretty, and above all seems to have a very sweet disposition ; she is quite well-educated, and a good judge of people and things, although she talks little. But I believe I know how to bring her out. Do you think her seriously ill? It would be so sad at her age."

" Well," he said, " she does not give me that impression at all. When she first came here she was very pale, but since, don't you think there has been a veritable resurrection? In less than two months her color and strength have returned. She no longer needs the carriage and Cadet to take her for the ozone. She walked with us very well for two hours yesterday in the pine woods. I believe that many young girls pass through such a crisis, especially if some love affair is mixed up with it, as, after what you have told me, I judge is the case with your friend's — our friend's daughter."

"Yes, all that usually disappears after marriage," said Madame Ferrier thoughtfully.

They were silent for a time, after which she asked :

"You have perfect confidence in Doctor Bar, have you not?"

He replied :

"Perfect confidence. Why?"

She hesitated :

"Because for the past week he has been watching and studying the child at length, and each time he gives her more reassuring hope."

Monsieur Perrier said :

"Well, Bar is too honest a man to promise a cure that he is not able to effect, or to declare a better state of health than he knows exists."

She seemed to be listening to a voice

within ; it seemed almost an effort for her to free herself from her thoughts.

"My old friend confided to me yesterday that the doctor assured her that Minnie had nothing to fear from her lungs or her heart, contrary to what her physician in Paris, her mother, and herself feared, — nothing, absolutely nothing. The respiratory troubles from which she has suffered for a time proceed solely from a nervous disorder, easily curable with ozone, water-cure, and especially by taking up her mind, — diversion and gayety. He repeated exactly what you have just said, that a happy marriage with one she loved would cure her."

"Upon my word," said Monsieur Ferrier, "although you may think me presumptuous, Bar's judgment does not surprise me at all. I have never believed that Mademoiselle Rugles had any serious trouble at all."

"Would you run the risk, Henri?"

"What do you mean, my dear?"

She did not reply at once, and seemed perplexed. Walking together slowly, arm in arm, they had strayed from the house, and

found themselves isolated in their large
garden sloping down towards the sea.

."Do you think," she asked, beating about the bush in truly feminine fashion, " that this child's heart has been affected so seriously that she can never forget her first painful experience? She loved her cousin, after all."

He said with a smile :

"I am not deeply versed in the psychology of young ladies. It seems to me, however, that Mademoiselle Rugles will do like many others who have loved a man they could not marry, she will marry some one else, whom she will love just as well, if not better. That will depend on the husband she has."

"But," said his wife, who seemed to be struggling against the invasion of a tempting but imprudent idea, " you must understand that a family might hesitate to marry a son to a delicate young girl. Would you feel safe in giving your son to her, even if she pleased you very much, if the family — as is the case — were perfectly honorable ; would you not be afraid, really, of what the future might have in store? "

Monsieur Ferrier looked more serious, but less surprised, than she had expected, smiling all the while.

"I admire your imagination, my dear. Is it a romance or reality that you are supposing? For, if I understand you, your determination to have Raymond established is always on your mind, and you were thinking of him this very moment."

"Do you disapprove of me, Henri?" she asked in a tone of tender anxiety. "Do you not feel concerned, as well as myself, about the life he leads, healthful, I admit, but empty and contemplative? Would you not like to see him married to a simple-hearted, good, upright young girl? Wait, my dear; in reality, I do not know what I ought to hope or fear, whether I am right or wrong in having imagined this romance and in not regretting that it cannot be a reality. Advise me, Henri; what do you think I ought to do?"

"Wait, my dear, and let things take their course. As for the young girl, if necessary Bar will tell us the real truth; there is no

professional secret which cannot be revealed
in certain cases."

He pressed Madame Ferrier's hand gently,
and added, teasing her affectionately :

"But, Némie,"— he often used this familiar
diminutive, — "in this...romance — for at
present it is one, is it not? — I am surprised
that you have not even asked whether Raymond would find Mademoiselle Rugles to his
taste."

"Ah!" she said, with a sigh, "if he is to
love her it will be right away or not at all.
But will he be able to love her? Do you
see any objections?"

Monsieur Ferrier repeated again :

"Wait, there is no hurry about it."

They went back into the house quietly,
arm in arm, without saying anything more
about the matter, both absorbed in thought.
She was surprised, and one might say hap-
pily disappointed, that her husband did not
make more objection to her suggestion, but
he was very reserved about everything con-
cerning his step-son and step-daughters, and
was much more lenient towards them than

towards his own sons, whom he was bringing
up very strictly. He smiled at his wife's
imaginations, only half believing in them,
without condemning them either, and saying
nothing against them, in order not to give
them the power of resistance, as almost
always happens with women, even the best.

Madame Ferrier went into the house and
bade the servants put her son's room in order.
She examined the linen in the drawers and
set fresh flowers on the mantel. The joyful
surprise she felt at expecting him that very
evening was mingled in her mind with a
rather nervous agitation, owing to the conversation she had just had. Serious doubts
tormented her; the more she felt that a marriage between Raymond and Minnie would
be dangerous, the more, according to the
illogicalness of human desire, she wished that
this dream might be realized. And yet why
not? But as soon as her hope took shape,
she put it away from her, preferring to consider it as something past, as a happiness
which might have been, if...

Certainly, when she recognized the friend

of her youth she did not expect that her old
affection would revive from its very roots,
grow green and vigorous, and put forth so
beautiful and rich a blossoming of memories,
harmony of ideas, and mental sympathy. She
began to love again with a very rare fresh-
ness of soul, a perfect and generous affection,
giving herself up entirely, remaining the
same good, spontaneous Noémie that Madame
Rugles had known and loved long before.

Moreover, she was not satisfied with reviving the intimacy of friendship and confidence with her, but she opened her heart
to Jean and Minnie ; they were not only
Helen's children, but it seemed as if they
were almost her own. And thus it happened,
in the warm return of this autumnal affection,
perfectly happy as she was in this unexpected
reunion with beings who responded fully to
her nature and feelings, that she had gone
so far as to cherish the regret, and from the
bottom of her heart indulge the persistent
and disputed unacknowledged and hesitating wish, for a union between her son and
the daughter of her fast friend. For just as

affection is not measured by the degree of relationship, and as those nearest us may have nothing in common with us, and may remain as indifferent to us as strangers, so this friendship of youth, interrupted for so many years, and renewed, by a surprising chance, at the same point as if their minds and hearts had developed in parallel channels up to the time of their meeting again, this friendship was to her the best of all, and preferable to other friendships that had been more constant and continuous; indeed, reciprocal suffering had purified it, no jealousy or petty feelings of ill-will peculiar to young women had come across it, and it was free from selfishness, broadened and enhanced by the age of wisdom which the two mothers had attained, and by their common anxiety of maternal love.

There was a rap at the door of her room.

"May I come in?" asked a voice that she recognized, as she hastened to open the door.

"Ah! Helen, is it you? How charming of you to come and surprise me! You have anticipated me, for I was just going to put on a wrap and go informally to invite you to breakfast to-morrow. My son is coming this evening, and I want you to know him. But what is the matter? Are you in trouble, my dear friend?"

And she took Madame Rugles's hands anxiously, for her face showed signs of painful emotion, her cheeks were on fire, her eyes filled with troubled tears.

"Ah!" she stammered, "my dear friend, it does me good to be near you! I came instinctively to confide in you; I will not conceal it from you, I am in great trouble; it was so unexpected...."

Two tears, standing in her eyes without dropping, rolled slowly down her cheeks; it was so sad to see these tears on the face of an old friend, to see a woman so courageous shedding them that Madame Ferrier, very much touched by these tears so unusual and restrained, made her sit down and, still holding her hands, asked her:

"Minnie is not ill? I noticed the doctor just now. It seemed to me that he was coming out of your house. It is not that which troubles you?"

Wiping her eyes, Madame Rugles replied:

"She is very well, too well. No, Doctor Bar, on the contrary, has given me every hope! But if she should have a relapse when she knows.... Perhaps she has had some hope; she never speaks of her cousin, but would she have recovered so quickly if in her heart she had not had some hope? I ask myself this with a pang, and it is this that makes me despair! If she were to be frightfully grieved! Just imagine it! Her uncle Davenne writes me that Guy is to be married! He was engaged day before yesterday. The marriage will take place in a month. Oh, my brother has lost no time," she said, with a bitter sneer; "that may be called a marriage by steam! Naturally, it is a fine match; she has a large fortune," her friend pressed her hand tenderly, "grand relatives, expectations! Wait, read his letter. I have just this moment received it; it upset me so that I took refuge with you. Fortunately Minnie was not in

the garden; Jean was there, and I could not
conceal the truth from him. He was indignant. I hope he will not let his sister notice
it. She is **too** bright not to suspect something in that case, and then!...

"It is not," she added with bitterness,
"that I felt **sorry** about his marriage.
Guy was not seriously in love; a **boy so** soft,
so incapable of resistance, would never have
had energy enough **to win** and defend his
happiness.

"But she, the poor little girl! Forgotten
in so short a time, forsaken, scorned, seeing
a stranger preferred before her, a rich, im-
pertinent minx whom Guy may have seen
three or four times;—a marriage arranged
by **worldly go-**betweens, **a** marriage of reason, money, **a** fine marriage indeed!" she
repeated with exasperated irony. "Ah! I
never knew my **brother till** to-day! He
was so anxious to see us go south. I am no
longer surprised **at it!** On his return from
America **Guy** found everything ready for
him, a wife, the contract and dowry, he had
nothing to do but say yes. Well, it is dis-

gusting ! There is something low in this way of treating us ! After my brother's refusal, they might have waited, for decency's sake ; a few months would have been no more than proper. But to hurry off this marriage, in order to put an end to the matter, to win Guy away from his first love, to write me this brutal letter, without any regret, without excuse, — ah ! I feel as if I detested them all. My brother, my sister-in-law, and my nephew are all odious to me ! This was stifling me, my dear Noémie, and I had to tell you about it ! Read his letter, read it, you will understand what they are ! "

A hurried step glided along the hall, a light tapping was heard at the door.

" What is it ? "

Madame Ferrier opened the door a very little way, and a chamber-maid replied :

"Madame, Monsieur Jean has sent the maid to tell Madame Rugles that Monsieur and Madame Essler have come to call upon her. Monsieur Jean and mademoiselle will entertain her while they wait for her."

Madame Rugles threw up her hands in

despair, with that comical violence with
which one receives an absurd and ridiculous
interruption unexpectedly occurring in the
drama of real life. "Say that I am out,"
she replied dryly.

But the chamber-maid came back to say:

"The maid begs to say that Monsieur
Jean has told Madame Essler that madame
is here, and that he would send for her."

"Very well," she said, and turning to her
friend added:

"Keep this letter, you may give it back to
me this evening. But no, you are expecting your son. We shall not be able to talk.
What do you advise me to do? To say
nothing to Minnie yet, do you not? Pro-
vided that she does not suspect anything?"

"Your eyes look red," said Madame
Ferrier. "Bathe them in my dressing-room,
put on a little rice powder! No, don't
say anything to your daughter. Who knows
—perhaps she will not feel as badly about
her cousin as you fear? And, between our-
selves, she will be quite right."

"Good-by," said Madame Rugles hastily,

and shrugging her shoulders with vexation added :

" I have little heart for receiving the Esslers ! "

" Listen," said Madame Ferrier, with a sudden inspiration ; " come this evening and take tea with me, if it is only for a moment. It is very mild, and if Minnie is well wrapped up she will run no risk."

" No, no, you will have your son ; we should be in the way ! "

" Exactly ; Raymond will be delighted. Do not stay with your sad thoughts this evening ; promise me to come, my dear friend, you know how fond we all are of you here ! "

They kissed each other hurriedly, and as their arms were disunited, their hearts impelled them to one more fond embrace.

V.

MINNIE, while changing her dress, happened to be standing behind the curtain of the window in her room, on the first floor. Her mother was talking with Jean in the garden. The postman had just come in and left a letter. Madame Rugles recognized the writing, tore it open and read it hastily, much disturbed ; then looking around her and raising her eyes to Minnie's room, she crumpled the paper and put it into her pocket.

She seemed to refuse to answer the questions Jean asked. Minnie guessed that she was divided between her desire to read the letter and fear of being overheard. Almost immediately she saw her disappear behind a clump of trees, still followed by Jean. Her dress, appearing and disappearing along the walks, stopped in front of the little gate at the end of the garden, and passed into the street that they often took to go to the Ferriers' house. Jean came back alone, his eyes fixed on the house, preoccupied and distrustful.

Minnie had no intention of watching them, and the idea did not even occur to her at first that they wished to conceal something from her ; but Jean's behavior, the mystery of the letter, her mother's furtive disappearance, aroused her curiosity, her suspicions, the consciousness of danger, and the unreasonable certainty that the danger concerned her. Bad news, loss of money ! The idea occurred to her, but she didn't

attach any importance to it. Why did they
look so uneasily towards her room, unless
they felt troubled, unless they had fears on
her account, unless they wished to keep the
truth from her? She grew pale.

" Has something happened to Guy? "

From the depths of her benumbed affection, from the days gone by, of which she
thought without hope and with resignation
mingled with lassitude, from the dead past,
for which she wore mourning, her cousin
came back to life again, with his velvety,
mild eyes, his thin face, timid grace, his tall,
rather awkward form. An accident? A fall?
Some illness? She was frightened, but more
by the idea than by the nervous sensation
which this supposed misfortune caused her.
A vague intuition whispered to her that none
of these things had happened to Guy. And
yet it was evident, from the trouble shown
by her mother and brother, by the disturb-
ing secrecy of that letter, that some misfortune was hovering over her. All her blood
rushed to her face.

"Guy is going to be married ! "

Then this explained all, and it could be
explained only in this way. A look of indig-

nation in Jean's features came back to her
then, and confirmed her clairvoyance. She
repeated :

"He is going to be married ! that is clear."

And as she had not finished dressing, she noticed that her arms were bare, and mechanically put on a waist, and buttoned it with a sort of modesty, with a shrinking gesture; her heart was cold. Why was she not more astonished, indignant, why did she not suffer more? But she knew that her suffering was made up of the distressing uncertainty, the confused stupor of the void into which she felt herself falling, while the furniture and the walls began to whirl around. She closed her eyes.

" He is going to be married. Well, then what?"

This only half shocked her; was she expecting it? A little sooner, a little later!... For a long time she had felt no hope. Guy's silence, his evasive and almost shameful attitude towards her while so far away, her uncle's determined, proud character, her aunt's crafty, unfeeling opposition, — all these signs had spoken with cruel eloquence. She repressed an artificial, painful laugh; the distress which bewilders feeble souls, meanly deserted, envelops them in darkness, cold,

and mental misery. But, at the same time,
a pride within her protested against the in-
justice of life, the nobleness of having nothing
with which to reproach herself, the voluptuous
satisfaction, intensified by a little vanity, of
being sacrificed, of being pitied, of meriting
the interest and warm affection of her own
friends. She tried to assure herself that she
did not suffer in her affection, that Guy was
a stranger to her, that without doubt it
was her self-love alone which bled. But did
it really bleed? She asked herself this, saying over:

"But I do not suffer; I would not have
believed that I should suffer so little."

At the same time she longed to burst into
tears, to take refuge in loving arms; she
wished that her mother were there and that
she might know everything from her, for after
all, in spite of the obstinate belief which
became plainer every moment in her mind,
there was nothing to prove that she might
not be mistaken. The thought of an accident recurred to her: Guy ill, Guy wounded,
perhaps in a duel. She fancied herself bend-

ing over his bed, caring for him. He came
back to life, recognized her with a faint
smile, her uncle and aunt Davenne smiled,
and their marriage was decided upon to take
place as soon as Guy should be well ; for their
wedding journey they would go to Italy.

She stopped short :

" Ah, me ! How crazy I am ! "

She could no longer bear not to know ; she
hurried down the stairs, Jean's name on her
lips, ready to call him ; but as she was going
into the garden a landau stopped before the
gate, the Esslers stepped out ; she was
taken aback.

The Esslers, puffed up with importance,
like their horses with their shining coats,
like their fat coachman with top-boots, had
no desire to go away. Jean in confusion
hastened to meet them, lost his head, and
sent for his mother.

The Esslers sat down in the drawing-room,
and Madame Essler complimented Minnie
because she was looking so well, while her
husband inspected the furniture, the imitation
Oriental carpet, the candelabra of gilded

zinc, the empire lithographs, the vulgar interior of this rented house ; he seemed to be comparing it with the furnishing of his own villa, which he let too, and as dear as possible to strangers.

"I have come to give your mother a scolding," said Madame Essler; "we never see her at Valençor, and yet I know that she makes calls and that you see people, the Silleroys, the Hawkinses, — charming people, are they not?"

But she did not mention the Ferriers, since she was jealous of the affectionate way in which they had monopolized the Rugleses, angry with them because they had taken them under their protection, and introduced them to the best society in Saint-Frégose. She brought the conversation round to Minnie's health, showing surprise that she had not chosen the old Doctor Sarrazin for her physician, assuring her that he had been mortified and pained by it. Madame Rugles appeared.

Jean and Minnie instinctively took advantage of this interruption to look at each other,

eager to read each other's faces, impelled
at exactly the same moment by an electric
communion of their thoughts. They both
felt troubled, and Minnie, dying to know
what it was, studied, as far as the conversation would allow, the constrained expression
of her mother's face and voice, Jean's uneasy
manner.

Exasperated by the prolonged stay of
these intruders, whom he mentally wished to
the devil, Jean began to move his foot uneasily,
which Monsieur Essler finally noticed; perhaps guessing the cause in this unsympa-
thetic atmosphere, he could not help turning
his eyes to the restless foot, and then looking
away towards the garden, with offended and
politely scornful haughtiness.

Madame Essler talked in a tone of friendly
volubility, jumping from one subject to another without allowing any one to come to a
conclusion or form an opinion about anything
whatever. The irritating triviality of her conversation, in the Rugleses' state of mind, cost
them a great effort to reply. At last she rose
and they escorted them to their carriage.

Monsieur Essler turned to examine the house :

" Isn't it damp ? " he asked. " No ? I should have thought it would be. It seems so."

" The Ferriers told us about it," said Madame Rugles. " We like it very much."

But they did not notice the remark, and went away, after making them promise to come to breakfast with them while the Flassmans were at their house, as they would be charmed to make their acquaintance.

The coachman started up the horses, which turned around prancing, and trotted away at a rapid rate. The Rugleses went into the house, and Jean announced with irony :

" Well, mamma, they are more friendly than they were the first day, but they are vexed all the same ; did you notice it ?..."

His eyes followed his mother's, and turned towards Minnie, who looked very pale, and was standing so motionless that she seemed rooted to the spot.

" Dearie," said her mother softly. She

came to her with a start, the color rushing
to her cheeks.

"The postman came to-day, didn't he,
mamma?" she asked.

Madame Rugles hesitated, too frank to
tell a lie; the strange tone of her voice
made her fear some snare.

" I think so, yes."

"Was it a letter from my uncle or my
aunt that you were reading, mamma?"

Madame Rugles turned crimson, opened
wide her eyes with despair and alarm; she
looked at Jean reproachfully; it was touching and ridiculously awkward.

" Jean has said nothing to me," Minnie
quickly declared. " I saw you reading a
letter in the garden. I was in my room; your
manner puzzled me; I wasn't thinking of
anything. Why do you look at me like that,
mamma? I am braver than you think. My
cousin is going to be married, isn't he?"

Madame Rugles put her hands on her
shoulders and drew her towards her, kissing
her again and again. Minnie did not cry,
she could not; her mother's mute, pathetic

impulse, instead of bringing her into sympathy with her, paralyzed her; unable to control her curiosity, she continued:

"Whom is he going to marry?"

Madame Rugles stammered:

"My dearie, forget it, forget all about it. We love you; be brave, think of the happiness which will some day make up for all this. You are so young. There, you deserve to be happy, and you will be. Promise me to try to keep well for my sake, for your brother's sake. We suffer so much on account of your grief."

Minnie smiled sadly.

"I am not jealous, mamma, I am not angry with him. I hope he will be happy, and "— her voice trembled a little as she declared — "I believe I am sincere in saying this; so you may tell me whom he is to marry. Is it some one whom I know?"

"No, I do not think so, my child. I do not know these people, the Bargeots, — manufacturers, I think."

She said this with the tip of her tongue, as if the words burned her on account of

the harm they would do her daughter. Jean,
heavy-hearted, bit his lips from vexation at
his helplessness. But Minnie, looking quite
calm, repeated :

" The Bargeots? No, I do not know
them. Are they rich people?" she asked.

" Rich," repeated the echo with indig-
nation.

" When is the wedding to be ? "

" In a — month ! "

One would have supposed that her mother
felt the greatest grief. Her voice trembled.

" Did Guy send me any message?"

She took her daughter's hands eagerly,
and her silent dismay was sufficient answer.

" No?" asked Minnie persistently, with
a touch of sarcasm. " Well ! I have more
courage than he has. I am going to let him
know, mamma, with only two words, that I
wish him much happiness ! "

Her voice broke, her face changed, grief
finally overpowered her.

" Dear me," she sighed, " what is the
use ? You will tell them, you, mamma. And
then..." the tears burst from her eyes,

"never speak to me about it again, let me
never hear him mentioned again, never!"

Madame Rugles drew Minnie to her, and throwing her arms about her with protecting pity said:

"Weep, my dearest, weep, but have faith in your youth, have faith in life, your old mother begs you to do so!"

Minnie sobbed in a low choking voice, as though the words were torn from her:

"Oh, mamma, I shall get over it, I shall get over it. I don't know why I am weeping!"

And yet she was weeping.

As he entered the Ferriers' drawing-room, Jean felt a warm, loving atmosphere about him. The lamps lighted up the friendly faces, and he saw only smiles, friends, and open hands. Merry children's voices bade him welcome. Madame Ferrier, agreeable and earnest, inquired:

"Where is your mother? And your sister?"

"They wished to be excused. Minnie is not quite well. They are very sorry."

She did not urge the matter, and leading him to a tall young man, who had been look-

ing at him with sympathetic curiosity ever
since he came in, she presented him:

"My son Raymond; our friend, Monsieur
Rugles."

Jean was at once charmed with Raymond's
face: he admired his high forehead with
closely cut hair; the bluish-gray of his eyes,
which assumed a tint of the wavering sea,
full of dreaminess, sweetness, reserve force;
his straight nose, and his mouth following
noble lines; his full blonde beard, wonderfully silky, framed the oval of his face and
fell down over his chest. In spite of this
beard like a Norman pirate's, he looked
young almost like a child, his sunburnt face
expressing the frankness and loyalty characteristic of sailor boys.

Colette, all daintiness, came to twine her
arms about her brother, her slender form con-
trasting with his broad shoulders and well-de-
veloped chest which the rough gymnastics, in
working his yacht, had given him; he placed
his hand on the child's hair, and Jean admired
the graceful firmness of his brown hand,
covered with golden down around the wrist.

"Monsieur Jean, **ask** Raymond **to** bring
his boat back soon, and take us all out sailing. Are you afraid of being ill? Yes? I
am never ill, and I love **so** much to dance
so," moving her hand up and down. "I
should have made a good sailor, shouldn't **I**,
Raymond?"

He smiled, **and** Jean noticed that this **tall**
fellow, with his formidable flowing beard cov-
ering his chest, was shy and not talkative;
this put him at his ease, and prevented him
from appearing awkward and stiff himself,
for usually **any new** face, **no** matter how
agreeable, embarrassed him. He was **re-**
assured **to** find Raymond **so** little **to be**
feared, but **at** the same time he felt charmed
and almost **awed** by this tranquil reserved
force, which, **in** the sober blue **of a** short
coat and duck trousers, seemed **to** keep **in**
the background, **to** retire **to** a corner of the
fireplace; his manner of walking noiselessly,
and speaking rather **low**, in a gentle, **caress-**
ing tone, pleased him.

"**Are** you **going** to remain for a few
days?"

"Oh! yes," exclaimed Colette, "he has promised to do so."

He replied:

"I shall remain, I think, two or three days."

She added, making up a little face, as though she had counted on his staying longer:

"To-morrow morning, he is going to tell the mother of one of his sailors about her son. Will you come with us? You will see the old quarter where the fishermen live."

"If you would like to have me, certainly!"

Jean looked for Madame Ferrier's approval as he said this. Then he smiled at Colette, aware that she was trying to make them friendly, her brother and himself, and very much taken with her, feeling indistinctly that he should fall in love with her if she were two years older; for although her fifteen years made her almost a young lady, yet her girlish slenderness made her seem to him like a little child. And yet neither Jeanne nor Andrée, who at that moment stood leaning over the back of their mother's chair, tall girls they were too, inspired in him the same feeling. Why was it? Yet they were as pretty as Colette, looking very much like her: Jeanne sprightly, Andrée a charming day-dreamer, always absent "in the moon."

Andrée was watching the clock attentively. The boys had already gone up to bed. The three sisters, who were preparing to follow, instinctively waited, their eyes coaxing to be allowed to stay up a little longer ; but it had struck ten ; according to their usual custom, they went to kiss Monsieur Ferrier first, then their mother, then Raymond. Colette's grasp of the hand which she gave to Jean was warm and hearty, her smile seemed more exquisite this evening, and so refined and delicately friendly that he was charmed by it.

" The delightful little girl !" he thought, following the light motion of her skirt as she disappeared like a fairy.

He did not dream that this "little girl" already knew more about life than he did, thanks to a gift of divination, of prescience and feminine observation, which he never suspected. He thought her too young for him and hadn't the least idea that he was too young for her, she was so much ahead of him in the proud superiority which he claimed for himself.

Madame Ferrier, noticing the mechanical gesture her son had just made, in carrying his hand to his coat-pocket and letting it fall immediately, murmured affectionately:

"Go and smoke, my dear Raymond; go, you are so unhappy without it!"

He blushed like a young girl discovered in a fault, and protested. His pipe, indeed, was his friend in his hours of solitude on the sea, and he had tried in vain to free himself from this slavery, to which he owed immobile dreams vanishing in smoke, the perfect happiness of a moment.

Monsieur Ferrier, understanding this, smiled, and lifting the shade at one of the glass doors showed the garden blue with moonlight.

"Come, let us go out there for a walk, and in this way, my dear, you will not be troubled by the smell of the smoke."

"But do you not smoke?" she asked Jean.

He understood that she would be glad to have him stay with her; he did not smoke except with others, through vanity not daring to acknowledge that the smell of tobacco made him ill.

When they were alone, as everything seemed to favor confiding in his mother's friend, and he felt that she was anxious about them, he explained:

"Minnie is not ill. Only she suspected what was in the letter mamma came to show you; it seemed that she saw us receive the letter and read it in the garden, and mamma did not dare deny the truth."

"The poor child!" said Madame Ferrier sympathetically. "Did she feel very badly? You, Jean, who know her so well and have her confidence, can judge."

He was flattered to have her appeal to his perspicacity:

"She wept, but my mother and I both expected her to show more violent grief. It is true she has great self-control; I left her quite calm. The dinner was not lively, but it was not so very sad either. If her health does not suffer in consequence, I have great hope. Oh! I am not sorry about Guy. Oh, no, good riddance to him! Oh! if Minnie could be loved by some good, noble fellow, she has everything to make him happy."

Madame Ferrier signed to him to lower his voice; the two men were passing in front of the window, and the gravel crackled under their feet.

"A noble fellow," she said thoughtfully, when their footsteps died away; "dear me, there are still such, fortunately."

She shook her head gently, a maternal tenderness giving her face a sympathetic, kindly charm.

"Will you tell your mother that I am sorry for her, and that I am grieved at her trouble? As for Minnie, say nothing to her. I will speak to her, or rather try to have her open her heart to me."

"Poor child!" she repeated.

They talked together for some minutes,

with confidential frankness. Suddenly Madame Ferrier asked :

" You like Raymond, do you **not?** I saw at once that you would be congenial. I should be glad if **he** might have you for a real friend."

He bowed, without noticing how cleverly she had put it; could she not really have wished him the good fortune **of** having Raymond for a friend, since he had everything to gain by it? But she had recognized, from the very first, a certain youthful conceit in him, and she humored him gracefully ; but this did not prevent **her** from loving all that was intelligent and good in him.

He replied :

" But I am quite ready to like him ! "

The two men soon returned. Madame Ferrier, all indulgence, said, smiling and slightly frowning, to her son :

" Well, did you have a good smoke ? "

VI.

As they were coming home from church the next day, all the Ferriers met Madame Rugles and her children on the walk by the seashore.

Raymond was presented to them.

Although Minnie was so absorbed in herself, she could not help noticing his diffidence, but as his diffidence was not lacking in manly grace and natural open-heartedness she was not displeased by it. He looked handsome in his loose, easy clothes, wearing, instead of a ridiculous stiff hat, a yachting cap of blue cloth.

He was not able to take her in at a glance, and judge of her as a whole and in detail, — a woman's glance, decided and unerring; he hardly dared look at her. He could not have told how she was dressed, nor what the shape of her face was; he saw only a graceful form, two lovely eyes, a refined, delicate expression of soul; this was all and enough; she pleased him. But he did not even know this, he did not formulate it at all in his mind, only feeling at ease in her presence, and free from dulness, — he who feared so much the embarrassment of social formalities. He thought it a beautiful day, that the bright blue sea beneath a sky of vivid blue and white was lovely to look upon, and he did not miss his boat, for he was as interested as a child in the rather unusual life in the streets this warm Sunday morning. Besides, Jean was at his side, whose presence could not fail to be agreeable to him.

"You would like to come with us, wouldn't
you, madame?" Colette asked Madame
Rugles. "If you have never visited the fishermen's quarter, you would see a part of Saint-
Frégose that you have never dreamed of."

Madame Rugles consulted Minnie :

"It would not tire you, would it, dearie?"

"Oh, no, mother, not at all!" she replied,
with a vivacity which did not exactly repel
the affectionate interest with which she felt
they all surrounded her, but it was restrained
by it, and kept them from noticing her, for her
modesty was alarmed at the thought of any
one knowing why she tried to conceal, this
morning, a sadness permeating her whole
being, the mental weariness resulting from
her experience of the day before. Moreover,
she was affected by her nervous, delicate
condition, which, it seemed to her, practised
eyes could read in her languid eyes, in her
pale features; at any time this idea made
her uneasy, even with her mother and her
brother. It gave her manner a particular
charm, both melancholy, discreet, and determined, showing the shrinking of a sensitive

soul, cowering with watchful eyes, vibrating at the slightest touch.

"But," said Monsieur Ferrier, "we are not all going to climb the old staircases; it would be like an invasion of the Saracens! Let us separate and meet again in the old port. Let those who like to walk fast come with me!"

The two boys placed themselves at his side; the two younger sisters hesitated, but a look from their mother decided them to remain with their father; Colette alone obtained permission to go with the Rugleses, her mother, and Raymond.

"Well, good-by for a little while!"

And Monsieur Ferrier walked quickly away with the four children towards the field of Argis, which they could see, ash-colored and reddish-brown, indented with pale olive-trees, relieved here and there by the dark-green tones of the underbrush of rosemary and rock roses.

At first the two mothers and the young people started along very slowly in a group together. People greeted them as they passed. They went under the railway-bridge, over which a train was rolling with a deafening rumble. In the avenue, on the right, was the station, the hotel omnibuses, coachmen and grooms in livery, leaning their elbows on the railing, stretching out their necks, their eyes and mouths wide open, like sharks ready to snap up a stray traveller.

The raw vegetables in a little market now filled the air with the odor of herbs and cabbage. Behind the little grove made by the four elms stood the dirty walls of the Hôtel de Savoie; Madame Loustigarel, in a white apron, standing in the doorway, courtesied in the distance, and the little humpback, seated on a post, smoking a cigarette, assumed a stiff, military attitude, putting his hand to his cap. This reminded the Rugleses of their arrival, and the mammas smiled at each other. Madame Rugles whispered:

"Oh! without you, Saint-Frégose..."

She added:

"But no, it is a charming, quiet nook! I have visited Cannes, in the times past, and Nice. The artificial life there, the faces of strangers, the continual coughing, the invalids, all made a painful impression upon me. Besides, it is so pleasant, so warm here, protected by the mountains. Why shouldn't I be grateful to a country which has so quickly restored my daughter?"

She sighed as she thought of her recent grief, and many things. Madame Ferrier understood, and said in a low voice:

"At her age, there is no such thing as irreparable sorrow."

And she smiled at the young girls, who, having gradually gone ahead, had stopped to wait for them. Raymond and Jean, who walked with longer steps, were some distance in front of them, in the bright sunshine, one with his broad shoulders, the other with his tall figure. They walked side by side through the dirty streets where the old town began, with lively, worn colors — green dregs of wine — canary yellow — of the shops belonging to the dealers in pottery and poultry, its inns for Italian masons, its out-of-the-way corners, where the head of some inquisitive old woman might be seen suddenly appearing from behind a shutter.

" There ! " said Colette. " Nothing has
changed here ; it is just the same to-day as
it was five years ago, before the new part was
built for the winter visitors. Look at all
those cats ! "

The farther they went along the paved
lanes, with their melancholy, soot-colored
walls, brightened up by an occasional window with a red geranium in bloom in the
midst of drying clothes, — the farther they
climbed towards the old church, the more
abundant became the cats of the poor
people ; at every door, crouching at the en-
trances to cellars, sleeping on the window-
sills ; gray cats with blue eyes, black ones
with green eyes, yellow ones with fawn-col-
ored eyes ; thin cats, fat ones ; filling this dead
quarter of the town, so that one might believe them to be almost the only inhabitants.
Timid dogs, however, showing less confidence than the cats, were digging with their
noses in the heaps of refuse, and fled at the
least sign of any one approaching. They
met an occasional fat Italian woman going to
the fountain for water, or a sailor, dried up

and tanned, nimbly climbing the flat, wide
stairs, the necessary ascent of which made
the ladies stop to consider.

"Now," said Raymond, who together with
Jean had turned back to join them, "you
will need courage; madame," he said to
Madame Rugles, "will you take my arm?"

"Thank you, sir, perhaps my daughter
will take it."

Minnie was on the point of refusing, but
he looked at her with a pleasant smile, and
she took his arm, leaning on it lightly.
Madame Ferrier, who remarked with a sigh
that she had no strength in her legs, ac-
cepted Jean's arm, while Colette and
Madame Rugles climbed the stairs bravely.

The steep steps, the ends of which were
formed with gray stones, were inlaid in the
middle with red tiles, which gave them the appearance of defaced mosaic, recalling the
appearance of one of those carpets which
only cover half of the stairs. Blue, soapy
water was running in a stream through the
gutters along the two walls; and between the
projecting tops of the houses, which almost

touched **each** other in places, as in the old
Arabian streets, appeared the bright, pure
sky, against which leaned the rough stone
tower **of** the old church. At last they
reached the landing, to Raymond's instinctive relief, and to his regret as well, for **he**
had found nothing **to** say **to** Minnie ; but he
missed the touch **of** her light arm as she
rested **it** on his, the frail touch, alive, maid-
enly, which the young girl, as soon as they
reached the top, released him from, thanking
him with a bright, fleeting smile.

" **Oh,** what a beautiful view ! " exclaimed
Madame Rugles. They were much higher
than they had expected to **be.** From there
they overlooked the great circle of the plain
of Argis, a stretch of country of reddish-brown
and soft tones, intersected by the silver furrow
of a winding **river.** At the foot of the platform were the crooked streets through which
they had passed. **Vast,** indefinite regions,
the new boulevard, the gleaming, sparkling
Casino ; on the left, villas amid masses of
verdure, and the sea stretching away, looking
as though it were lacquered **in the offing,** of

a duller blue in the bay. The mountains as
far as the end of the cape formed around
Argis and Saint-Frégose a triple rampart;
those in the foreground were green, while
those in the middle distance looked blue and

more indistinct, and those in the background,
gleaming in pale sheets, lifted their peaks
white with snow.

A deep silence, the calm splendor of
winter in the south, hovered over this happy
landscape, full of harmony, almost melancholy in its stillness. The old church, built

of yellow stones and cemented with red
mortar, of a peculiar picturesqueness, shared
in the beauty of the scene ; one of the sides
of the square tower was freshened by a gigan-
tic curtain of foliage which trembled in the
brisk air. The church was enlivened by an
old fig-tree which, growing out of the very
stone, and springing from one of the but-
tresses, five metres from the ground, put
forth its gray branches, the scanty leaves of
which stood out against the blue sky. This
church of the poor, so different from the
new church and the white town so neglected
and so quiet, perpetuating under the open
sky the symbol of its teaching through the
tenacious life of the stone and the tree, under
its clinging curtain of tropical creepers, impressed the Rugleses very much, and Minnie
especially.

She exclaimed :

" How peaceful it is ! And we have never
been up here before, mamma ! "

" Oh ! " said Colette, " mamma comes here
often to visit her poor people ! "

She bit her lips :

" I shall be scolded. Mamma doesn't like
to have any one speak of that, and she is
looking at me with such eyes, such eyes!"

"Who would believe," said Madame Ferrier, "that a big girl like you would be so
childish still!"

She was smiling, and everybody smiled.
Colette's only reply was suddenly to rush at
her and kiss her, almost knocking off her
bonnet.

Raymond looked stealthily at Minnie. She
was breathing with some difficulty, the climbing having fatigued her. Her face, which he
only saw from the side, seemed more pleasing
on account of it, her refined lips parted. He
feared she would be the worse for it.

"Let us not stay here, the air is rather
cool. Will you go into the church? It is
very modest, but we have been faithful to it,
and I believe," he said, with loving mischievousness, "that my mother sometimes comes
here to pray in secret."

He pushed back the swinging door, standing out of sight as he held it open; the
leather of it was very old, and the hair was

bursting through in places. He entered last
after Minnie. She dipped her fingers in the
holy water, and with a spontaneous, perfectly
natural movement held them out to him before crossing herself. This moist touch was
so imperceptible that he had to think a moment before realizing its sweetness.

A peaceful twilight enveloped them, and
their eyes, coming from the bright daylight,
could hardly make out the interior of the
church, to see how humble it was, worthy of
fishermen and old men from the hospital.
It was evident, at once, that it had been
deserted for the other, the new church ; certainly none came there but the lowest class
of people, the infirm, the wretchedly poor,
or those who were too old and too near
death to change the customs of a whole life-
time. The chairs, grayer than ashes from
secular dust, were badly worn, some of them
having nothing left but the empty wooden
frame. The altar, so rigidly clean and bare,
suggested primitive worship ; the confessional
was a simple brown oak board, perforated like

a skimmer, with round holes through which
the priest listened and answered.

In a tiny chapel, as dark as night, smiled
a massive, awkwardly stiff, ungilded virgin.
Some little wooden boats, like children's
toys, barks cut out with a sailor's knife, ships
rigged by rough fingers, hung suspended from
tarred cordage, as votive offerings. The incense burned at high mass smelled old, and
a night-light, probably relighted after it had
gone out, gave forth a musty smell of oil.
But the nave and the choir, such as they
were, impregnated with humanity, gave forth
the breath of prayer, the credulous innocent
faith, the very soul of these aged and childish
people. A warm and deeply peaceful atmosphere slowly took possession of their hearts ;
poor as the place was, they felt that they
were in the house of the good Lord.

The women knelt down, and the two
young men stood still, Jean looking at the
pretty outline of Colette's form, Raymond at
the stained-glass windows. From instinctive
delicacy he turned his head away from Minnie while she was on her knees, a look even

of sympathy seeming to him inconsiderate
when directed towards the prostrate form of
a woman in prayer, showing an indefinable
trust and touching fervor.

When they passed the holy-water basin
again, he gave back to the young girl the
holy water she had offered him.

When they came out the bright daylight
dazzled their eyes, and in spite of the splendor of the light he felt almost bewildered,
and supposed that Minnie was affected in
the same way, coming from the dim religious
shade where their thoughts must have been
in harmony. Their eyes met and then immediately turned away, as if this little simple
encounter were not according to the rules of
propriety. She blushed slightly, or rather
grew rosy, like the brightness of a flower,
for everything about her was so furtive, shaded
with such subtle tones, and the attractive mystery about her person was caused by such a
strange unrest and frailty, flashing and dying
away in electric pulsations of soul.

They did not go down the same way, but
by a winding path bordered by a parapet,

and following high, melancholy walls. The
descent was so steep that Raymond gave his
arm again to Minnie.

" In the first street, the corner of which you
will see a little farther down," he said, " lives
Aunt Goulette, my sailor's old mother. I am
going to tell her about him. Although he is
only an adopted son, she loves him passion-
ately. She speaks only a patois, so you will
not understand her; but her face is so ex-
pressive when talking about her boy that you
will make out what she is saying by merely
looking at her." ·

Colette had joined them.

"Oh! you know," she said, "that Aunt
Goulette's house is not exactly a splendid
place, for although my mother and brother
see that she doesn't need anything, she has
never been willing to give up her business,
which is not one of the choicest: she buys
rabbit-skins."

They came to a little, low house with a
narrow door. In a chair a paralyzed old
man sat warming himself in the only ray of
sunlight which fell aslant the dark street.

"You see this poor man," said Raymond
in a low voice ; "well, Aunt Goulette, who is
foolishly self-sacrificing, has adopted him
just as she adopted my sailor. She feeds
him and takes care of him."

He said good morning in reply to the old
man's feeble bow, and asked :

"Is Aunt Goulette there?"

At the same time he knocked on the door.
A very old woman appeared, with a muddy,
scarred complexion, and eyes almost blind ;
she wore on her head the large straw hat
customary among the peasant women. She
looked at Raymond and the fine company
he was with, lifted her arms in the air with a
sharp yet joyful and plaintive *Moun Di,*...
her faded eyes brightening and the suggestion of a blush coloring her old cadaverous
face. The sing-song accentuated Provençal
syllables poured from her mouth. Colette
translated them to Minnie.

"She doesn't ask us to come in, because
she says that her rabbit-skins are not accustomed to receive such fine visitors. You
see she is speaking about her son ; she is

asking when he is coming home. She is calling him 'Mon beü Marius.' She is asking
if he is well."

She added :

"It is true that these rabbit-skins..." and
she drew Minnie back a little, in reality to
allow her brother to give some money to the
old woman without any one seeing him.
She refused it, declaring she had everything
she needed. He urged her to take it, saying :

"It is from Marius. It is his pay. He
wished me to give it to you."

And he quickly started away to escape
Aunt Goulette's protestations. But she called
him back, and, smiling at Minnie, said something which the young girl could not understand : she only heard the words "poulido
damisello," pronounced with admiration.
The old woman had already disappeared in
the dark room, where they could see the
rabbit-skins hanging from the ceiling, and
strings of red peppers and onions. She
came back immediately, bringing a bunch of
fresh pinks, which she had taken out of a

glass of water. She offered them to Raymond with some words of her patois, looking at Minnie with a kindly old woman's smile.

Colette explained :

"She begs you to accept these flowers. She is sorry that she hasn't enough for all of us. She offers them to you because this is the first time she ever saw you, and because you are as pretty as 'oune fiançade' — as pretty as a bride."

"Thank you," said Minnie, "thank you," and she took the pinks from Raymond, and, smelling of them, said : "They smell good, very good."

The old woman shook her head vigorously, smiling with her toothless mouth ; the paralytic smiled with interest also ; and on these two earthy faces it was like a ray of light breaking over old ruins.

"Good-by," said Raymond ; "au revoir !"

The descent continued very steep towards the open country, ending in an avenue of plane-trees to which a few copper-colored leaves still clung. A sound of running water gurgled in the gutter, and a washerwoman's bat, as she crouched down, dipping her linen in the clear stream, cut the smiling sleepiness of the morning. They could see the river better, beyond smooth meadows furrowed by canals; it wound along between tamarinds, tufted reeds, and rushes. And suddenly the little harbor came in sight, and the infinite sand beach, stretching along like a giant sickle as far as the cape, where the foreground of the mountains was lost in the promontory.

"What a charming little corner!" said Minnie, pointing with her parasol towards the harbor. "We never had a suspicion of it, had we, mamma?"

It was a small village square, planted with mulberry-trees; lines were stretched from one tree to another, and on these the fishermen's linen was drying; a quantity of boats drawn up on the sand lined the curve of the harbor, a child's harbor, which seemed hardly large enough to hold a single large boat, and which two little breakwaters on a rocky formation held like crabs' claws.

A lighthouse overlooked the one on the left, on which two custom-house officers with rhythmic step were walking up and down, with their hands in their pockets. At the end of the one on the right stood Monsieur Ferrier and his children, and a band of urchins were running with all their might over the even unbalustraded stone blocks, flying a kite. One of them stumbled, almost fell off the jetty on the rocks below which supported it, on a level with the water.

" Dear me !" exclaimed Madame Rugles, but the rogue clung with his hands and knees as supple as a kitten, jumped up and ran to overtake the others.

" Really," she added, " I was frightened. I do not understand how the mothers of those children can let them run about so near the water, an accident could happen so easily."

"There are Jeanne and Andrée motioning to us," said Colette. "Let us go to them."

"Oh !" said Madame Ferrier, "I don't like to see them there very well; I am not going there, and we should do much better to wait for them here."

"But, mamma, what danger do you think there is? The breakwater is as wide as a road."

"Well, go, but don't be careless," and Madame Ferrier remained with her friend on the beach, watching a fisherman sitting on the ground mending his net, while Raymond, Minnie, Jean, and Colette ventured on the thick ribbon of stone. On the right and on the left masses of rocks enlarged the course of masonry, plunging into the transparent green or the opaque blue water. The two parties were already meeting, and Jacques and Lucien were running ahead of the others, when sharp cries were heard. Jean and Raymond turned round in alarm, only to see the band of rascals coming towards them as fast as they could run, the kite having flown away, pitching headlong into the sky.

The one who was holding it turned around to look at it; a misstep in his blind chase threw him out of a straight line; he stepped off, fell on the rocks, and with one splash tumbled into the water without letting go the string, which he dragged along with him.

An outcry of dismay, ohs, ahs, exclamations of *Bon Diou*, cries of terror from the two mothers on the shore, all took but a moment. A second plunge scattered drops of sunshine in the air, the water in the harbor moved in wide eddies, a dark body went down into the depths, they saw nothing but the blue sheet of water, and only then they realized, the thing had happened so quickly, that it was Raymond who had just jumped into the water with his clothes on.

The frightful silence of suspense petrified the Ferriers on the spot, Jean, Minnie, and the children ; nothing was heard but cries of despair from Madame Ferrier, who was nailed to the beach with fear. The fisherman who had been mending his net ran with all his might ; in the midst of inexpressible anguish, the dark, moving body reappeared under the water, and they saw beneath a face dripping with water, a beard drenched with water, two arms clasping a lifeless bundle. The fisherman, bending over the rocks, seized the child, and Raymond, catching hold of the rough places, caught his breath, then with Monsieur Ferrier's assistance climbed up with difficulty, under the weight of his wet garments, slipping as if the sea were pulling him back. He rubbed his shoulder, and when his step-father threw his arms around him, saying, " What a fright you have given us ! " he made a grimace as though he were in pain.

" Are you hurt ? "

" I think not. I struck my shoulder on a rock ; that pains me a little, but it is of no consequence."

" Your poor mother ! "

Raymond passed his hand over his face, wrung out his beard like a piece of cloth, shook his hands, and without looking at anybody ran to his mother, whom Madame Rugles was supporting, and who, midway on the breakwater, was tottering and seemed ready to faint.

" Oh, my son ! my son ! "...

" What you did was fine," exclaimed Madame Rugles, enthusiastically ; " but imagine your mamma's feelings ! I was frightened ! "

People came running and surrounded them ; windows were thrown open ; exclamations were made around them.

" How is the child ? " asked Raymond, looking about for him.

" He is alive, Monsieur Ferrier, he is alive ! " exclaimed the head officer, running to him ; " they have just taken him into the guard-house, and are taking care of him. He was full of salt water, the poor little fellow ! "

And this man, who wore on his breast a military medal and the cross of the Legion of Honor, an old soldier with his face scarred by a sword-cut, added :

" Monsieur Ferrier, will you do me the honor to allow me to press your hand? But do not stay here, come into the guard-house ; a glass of brandy will revive you ! "

" No, no, " said Raymond, " I only need to change my clothes ! "

" Have a carriage, monsieur ? " exclaimed one of the hack-drivers attracted to the spot with the rest of the crowd, and pointing to his coupé in waiting.

"Get in, my son, get in quickly. I will go with you; you need warm clothing."

"Wait," said the chief officer; "at least you shall wrap my cloak around you."

He brought it out quickly from the guard-house, compelled Raymond to let him throw it over his shoulders, and he, anxious to escape from the comments of the people, the cries of the women, the congratulations of the officers, could not help asking once more :

"The child is in no danger, is he?"

"Pshaw! To-morrow he will be running around as usual, with his kite!" said the brigadier.

"But he didn't let go the string!" declared the fisherman, adding: "Oh! here comes his mother running! And his uncle! They want to thank you, monsieur!"

Other voices exclaimed :

"Here comes the doctor!"

"Come, Raymond, come!" repeated Madame Ferrier, distracted and almost be-

side herself with pleasure and fear; if her
son should take cold in his lungs, now! He
was equally anxious to get away from the
grateful parents; he helped his mother hastily
into the carriage, and jumped in after her.

Then, escaping from the crowd of people,
Madame Rugles and Monsieur Ferrier looked
at each other. Monsieur Ferrier was pale,
Colette sobbing convulsively, the other children all deeply agitated.

"Come," he said, trying to recover his
presence of mind; "let us go home! It has
all ended well."

He laughed a little nervous laugh, trying
to regain his liveliness and failing to do so.
The shock was still of too recent occurrence.

Madame Rugles, much affected, remarked:

"All in a moment! All in a moment!
It passed like a dream! Oh, what a brave
soul! You are proud of him, are you not?"

She drew near to her daughter, who said
not a word; her eyes were dim, her breath
almost taken away, her face as pale as wax.

"You were very much affected, weren't
you, dearie?"

Minnie made no reply; her fingers trembled, her lips quivered. Colette put her arm around her waist, and, shaking all over with convulsive emotion, exclaimed:

"Oh! have I not good reason for loving my Raymond?"

She added in a lower voice:

"You will be fond of him too, won't you? What he did was so fine!"

VII.

" Aren't you asleep, Minnie? "

They slept in the same room, and Madame
Rugles, who was a light sleeper, had just
awakened a few moments after her daughter,
aroused by a change in her breathing, which
sounded less regular and at the same time
stronger, by a rustling of her hands under the
sheet, by an indefinite moving about to find
a cooler spot.

" No, mamma."

" You are not feverish, I hope."

" No, mamma."

A long silence followed, dominated by the trembling obscurity of the room, lighted with a night-lamp, the hallucinating appearance of the furniture, the unformed apprehension in their eyes, trying to penetrate the dark corners, the uneasiness of the gloomy hour, when one feels not quite secure against an invasion of thieves and murderers, when one's thoughts assume the coloring of a nightmare, and, dreading sterile sleeplessness, long to see the pale dawn light up the windows.

Hearing them stir, the little life rolled up in a ball on a cushion began to stretch ; the black kitten uttered a feeble mew, arched his back like a camel, stretched himself out like a rabbit, licked his fur, gathered himself into a heap, and with one bound jumped on Minnie's bed, rubbed his nose against hers, put his paws around her neck, nibbled her chin.

" Stop, Pierrot, stop ! "

Now he was pulling her hair, seizing hold of the lobe of her ear.

" Oh, how playful he is ! Go away, go and tease mamma ! "

"No, no," said Madame Rugles quickly, for she was afraid of cats, and only tolerated Pierrot for Minnie's sake. As Minnie drew her arm out of bed to caress the little creature, she said to her :

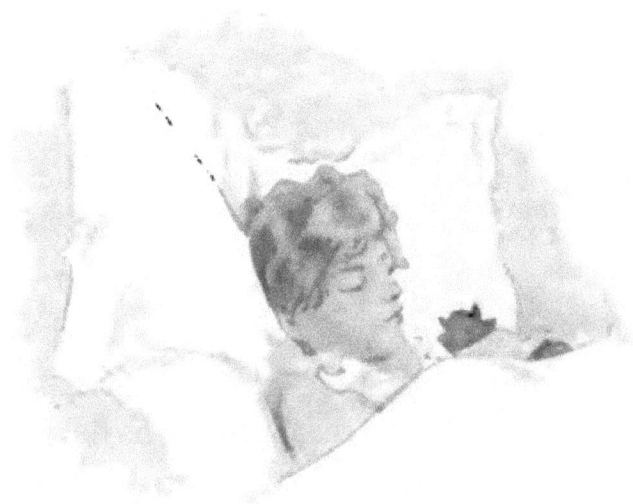

"Don't uncover yourself, you will take cold ; the nights are still cool."

She added :

"If you play with him, you will not go to sleep again."

"Do you feel sleepy?"

"Do I? No, my night is over," said

Madame Rugles. "But at my age, one doesn't require as much sleep. It is late, or, rather, very early. Go to sleep again, dearie, you need it."

"Oh! I am doing very well now," said Minnie.

"Yes, the ozone has done wonders for you, as well as the sunshine and the air. None of our friends will know you when we go back to Paris. Who would have thought in selecting Saint-Frégose, which we knew nothing about, and had no reason for coming to except on account of the Esslers, that we should find such a good climate for you, such excellent treatment, so perfect a physician, and such friends as the Ferriers?"

"It would be strange," said Minnie, "if Madame Ferrier should happen to be awake just now, as well as yourself. Imagine her feelings when she saw her son throw himself into the water!"

"I thought she would be insane. I knew how I should feel if it had been Jean instead of Raymond who had jumped into the water. Fortunately, he doesn't know how to

swim. But it makes a cold chill run down
my back to think of the misfortune that
might have happened."

Minnie replied :

"How simply he did it all ! How mod-
estly he stole away afterwards ! and all day
he seemed bored and annoyed by the praise
he received. Colette told me, after the third
visitor had come to compliment him, that
her brother had a mind to go away without
saying a word to any one, it troubled him so
much to receive so many congratulations."

"Yes," said Madame Rugles, "when the
mayor came in behalf of the municipality, he
replied : 'But I deserve no credit, I know
how to swim.' Nevertheless he might have
been hurt, or held under the rocks. Only
imagine what a misfortune it would have
been, or what would have happened if that
wretched little fellow had not been fished
out in time. It makes me tremble. Really,
there are no misfortunes which cannot be
overcome, or to which we cannot be resigned, except the death of one we love —
that is irreparable."

The tone in which she said this made
Minnie think of her father, whose poor re-
mains were buried under the earth in the
little cemetery at Mortefontaine, where they
had had him transported, that they might
feel nearer to him, in the summer put
flowers on his grave in a peaceful enclosure,
and not feel that he was lost in the crowd in
one of the great graveyards in the suburbs of
Paris.

By an association of ideas which she could
not help, she thought of Guy soon to be married, of her cousin now dead to her. She
thought of him without vexation, without
bitterness, with sad, but courageous, pride.
Why was it that then she seemed to see again
the young man whom she had met for the
first time the day before, with his manly bearing, his timid, honest eyes, the native nobility
of his character ; this Raymond, so different
from Guy that he seemed to have nothing
in common with him, either in looks, or in
mind or soul ? Why did she repeat to herself without attaching any deep meaning to
them — although she felt obscurely that they

had a meaning for her — those words of her
mother's :

" Only the death of one we love is irreparable ! "

She mechanically fondled the black kitten,
which, curled up in the hollow of her breast,
was purring in the warmth of her neck, and
she felt a pleasure in smoothing the velvety
fur, the warm coat of the contented animal.

" How old is Monsieur Ferrier? " she
asked suddenly.

" I don't know ; sixty-five, perhaps."

She replied, hesitatingly :

" No, I meant his step-son."

" Monsieur Raymond ; but he bears his
father's name, Monsieur Jermyn. He is
twenty-seven. He looks older, he is so
strong and robust."

Minnie did not answer ; what her mother
had just said corresponded to her own impression ; it was true that his calm, wise
force of character, little as she knew him, inspired her with confidence, an inclination to
trust in him, to feel perfectly secure when
by his side — a sentiment she had never felt

with Guy. But she went no farther, either because she was afraid of judging Raymond too generously and so soon, or because she did not wish to understand what she could not explain in herself, that which did not exist till the day before, and which, since she had seen him, and especially since she had feared for his life, troubled her in an incomprehensible and obstinate fashion.

She tried in vain to attribute her restless anxiety, her undecided obsession, to unusual nervousness ; to a condition which kept her agitated, accelerated the flow of her thoughts, intensified her sensibilities ; to the circulation of her blood, rushing to her temples and flowing back to her heart, giving her fits of dizziness or attacks of sick headache ; she admitted with extreme reluctance and unreasonable shame the presence within her of something or somebody unfamiliar, troubling her like a real, mysterious presence. Her sense of modesty revolted against the inexplicable subjection, but something strong and strange, nevertheless, held sway over her mind, her curiosity, her heart, her nerves, her hesitating senses, and aroused her maidenliness.

"What are you thinking of?" asked Madame Rugles, for this silence, so full of thought, made her fear, not what Minnie could not yet know herself, but one of those absorbing, distracting reveries which she did not like to have her daughter indulge in, because she was afraid she would not be able to follow her, or find her again afterwards.

"Are you asleep?" she asked again, after a moment, having received no reply.

"No," said Minnie slowly.

Madame Rugles did not press her further. The idea did not occur to her, in her innocent ingenuousness, that Minnie might possibly be haunted at that time by the reaction from that brutal emotion, the perilous and unexpected rescue, the risking of one life to save another. Besides, she believed that the young girl had no thoughts for any one but her cousin Guy. She did not suspect that Raymond could in any way whatever, through the insidious contact of pleasant daily intercourse, or in consequence of the fortunate drama of the day before, abruptly arousing the feelings and suddenly calling forth sympathy, — she did not suspect that Raymond could ever enter into their life.

Her honesty and a delicacy of feeling, rare in a woman having a daughter to marry and naturally anxious to establish her to the best advantage, would have prevented her, moreover, from allowing herself to hope for a possible union. She would have looked upon such a desire as not quite scrupulous on her part, and also as improbable, Minnie's dowry being too small in comparison with the young man's fortune.

Doubtless, however, if she had allowed herself to dream such a fine thing, or even to conceive it, she would not have been able to help a feeling of regret, although bearing her grief nobly; she would have perhaps sighed, for would it not have crowned all her hopes? But for the moment, she never thought of it; however, Minnie's meditative silence disturbed her; she asked again, quite softly:

"Are you asleep?"

And **very softly** came the reply :
" No."

"**She must be** thinking of Guy," thought
Madame Rugles, with a movement of anger
towards the Davennes, which made her mat-
tress creak under the weight of her large
body as she turned over. She noticed **then**
that the gray light **of** day was coming **in at**
the window, through **the** opening **of** the curtains.

Raymond, **who** rose very early, was already
dressed, and stood leaning his elbows on the
balcony by his open window, in the clear
fresh **air** of this winter springtime when the
earth smells good. **He** heard **a** knock at his
door.

His mother, in a wrapper, came in :

" Good morning, mamma. What **time is**
it ? "

" It is six o'clock. Everybody is still
asleep, but **I** have **not** closed my eyes all
night. I heard **you** open your blinds. I
couldn't wait any **longer.** I wanted to see
you."

She kissed him.

"You are not cold? You are sure you are not ill? Oh! my child, what you did was very fine, but you did not think that I might have had to mourn for you all the rest of my life. It seems to me now as if I should never be easy again when I know you are on the water. The very thought of your exposing your life again, of your risking it at any rate, of your striking against a rock and going to the bottom without having time to know what has happened [she shuddered, although, calm and reassuring, he held her in his arms and smiled], — no, I shall not live in the future! You are not going away, are you? You are going to stay with us a little while. I have seen you so little since yesterday, and for weeks you have been sailing far away from me. To-day again I shall not have you to myself, but I shall not be jealous. The Rugleses are very dear friends of mine, and I hope they will be yours too; I want to feel sure that it will not trouble you too much to spend the day with them."

In order to escape visitors and to recover

from the unforeseen accident of the day before, which had encroached a little too much
on their usual life, it had been decided that
the two families should start together in the
morning and go to breakfast at Toray, an
out-of-the-way place on the shore.

" No, why should it?" he asked.

She sighed :

" You are so shy, my tall Raymond !"

" What would you like? It is true, I do
not care for conventionalities which are more
or less hypocritical, calls, vain, jealous gossip.
I do not like young girls — oh ! I know very
well what you mean !— flirting young girls,
satisfied with themselves, looking for a husband, full of false sentimentality or false in-
nocence, or annoying with their impertinence.
But if a person is good and simple, I feel immediately attracted to her."

He flushed as he said this, and his mother
looked at him attentively, saying :

" Then Madame Rugles ought to please
you."

He replied :

" I don't know her well enough yet, but

the kindness of her face and her beautiful eyes speak in her favor."

" Her son is pleasing, isn't he ? — although he is at a thankless age, self-satisfied, anxious to make a good impression ; both awkward and forward, but he is a capable fellow. He likes you very much."

He bent his head with a smile.

" And Mademoiselle Rugles?" she asked indifferently.

He did not raise his eyes, and said with a simplicity which was rather more marked than usual, hesitating a little, at least so it seemed to his mother :

" Mademoiselle Rugles is not like the young girls I know."

" Do you mean better or worse ? "

He looked at her and reddened.

" I have not formed an opinion, mother, and because I have not ventured to form an opinion is the very reason why I think that she is different from others. When I am with her I feel intimidated, but not uneasy, however ; without feeling anxious to seem different from myself, and out of politeness to pretend to sentiments which I do not feel. I feel quite *myself* when I am with her; besides, I know that you would not all like this family so much, if they did not deserve it."

He spoke with a mixture of frankness and timidity, in a voice rather husky and naturally grave; it suited him well and gave a manly nobility to his features, at the same time his liquid eyes were like a child's, which no doubtful love had ever saddened or soiled.

"Do you know how handsome you are?" said Madame Ferrier. She had placed her hands on his shoulders and was admiring him with touching artlessness. "Tall as you are, I seem to see your father again, although he did not have your shoulders. What woman could help falling in love with you?"

"Mother, women are not as indulgent as you are. No one will love me as you do."

"That is very true, my son, but she will love you differently, and you will not love me as much. At least, may I see you happy! Your sisters will marry, and will leave the house empty. Your brothers will go away

for their education and their life work. I
shall grow old with the excellent man who
loves you so much ! And then it would be
very sweet if you should have children, to
remind me of the time when you were little !"

She laid her head on her son's breast, and
threw her arms around him :

" You are here, Raymond, you are alive,
thank God ! But since the horrible fright
you gave me, and which I do not reproach
you for, I cannot get over the idea that you
might have been lost. What insane ideas I
had last night ! Promise me that you will
stay more on land. Do you not get tired of
being away so long? Your life on the water
must be monotonous."

He did not reply, but kissed her on the
forehead ; they remained for a long time in
each other's arms, without speaking.

VIII.

RAYMOND and Minnie exchanged greetings without venturing to look at each other, or barely doing so. A bashfulness, developed in the night, had come over them. Does that mean that they were ill at ease? No, because they were happy, but did not dare to acknowledge it; victims of the charming awkwardness which a youthful reciprocal instinct causes in sympathetic souls, they were light-hearted and their manner seemed full of embarrassment.

What, so soon? Did Minnie disown her

stifled, wounded affection for Guy? No, her heart was full, she was in love, but she knew not with whom, and only knew that it was no longer her cousin. And Raymond? Had his rather timid candor forsaken him? Had he renounced his youthful, free independence? He did not admit this at all, only the sight of Minnie agitated him. He kept a little behind the others and furtively watched the swaying of her body as she walked, the light shadow she cast on the ground, or the healthful whiteness of her neck under the pale gold of her hair.

His agitation, which he could not explain, made him silent and quiet all the way, while the two families, with the shouting of the children, the smothered laughter of the older girls, the talk of the parents, went merrily down the steps leading to the little local railway which ran to Toray. As soon as they had taken up the two first-class compartments in the tiny train, Raymond tried to rouse himself, and in this way felt that he ought to speak to Minnie as he had done the day before. There was no objection to

it. What did he say, what words did he
use? He could not account for it, but, very
much confused to see her blush, he blushed
himself; was it timidity, or a delicate sympathy in a common feeling of bashfulness?

Then he felt the strange surprise which
the consciousness of the instability of the ego
gives us. Yesterday he was a calm, delib-
erate Raymond, strong and peaceful: to-day
he felt like quite another being, insecure,
uneasy, lacking in energy. It seemed as if
his resolution had vanished away; he felt
as weak as a child. Instinctively his eyes
would have been directed to Minnie; but he
did not carry out the inclination, for he
was so afraid of reading in her eyes that
too marked attentiveness was displeasing
to her. His desire to look at her was so
strong that he refrained from turning his
head towards her, riveting his attention ob-
stinately on the scenery, through which the
train was slowly passing, with long stops at
stations which looked like toys, boxes made
like little Swiss cottages, small enclosures
standing out by the side of solitary roads,

against a background of pine woods, or close
to the sea, on the very sand.

" What a beautiful morning ! " repeated
the merry voices around him. " What a
beautiful morning ! "

Oh ! yes, it was glorious, surely, and
warm, and the air so light and pure, divine
to breathe, and smelling of fresh aromas, the
red earth and the faint saltiness of the sea.

Raymond's heart suddenly expanded,
opening to an intense joy in living, to an indistinct, vague, immense hopefulness. He
desired nothing but to travel in this way forever. But, slow as the little train went
along, stopping in the midst of the woods,
letting off quantities of steam and blowing
long whistles, on the narrow road, like a real
train, at last it reached Toray, let them all
get out, and started on peacefully, so minute
with its three cars, into the wide country.

At the end of a winding path, among fields
of reeds, the few houses of Toray lifted their
tiled roofs, eaten by vegetable rust, and
covered with green and brown moss.

The sea surrounded it on two sides, on

one a sandy beach, the other a rocky shore
level with the water. The beauty of the day
seemed quite new to Minnie. Often, since
her rapid restoration to health, she had
admired the mild splendor of the Provençal
winter, had concentrated her inmost feelings
into these words: "How beautiful it is!
how good it is!" And yet it seemed to
her that this corner, which she had never
seen till to-day, revealed a still more beautiful aspect of things. A strange strength
contracted her muscles, she breathed with
joy, walked with a lively step, a sudden brightness lighted up her eyes. What was going
on within her? Was it only the happiness
of feeling herself well, or nearly so, the in-
toxication of a life still young, that is felt
when escaping from convalescence? Was
it more, a bubbling up of the sap, the blossoming of a loving soul, suffering with love,
eager to love?

She thought with inexpressible pity of the
sad invalids, whom she greeted now with a
little nod when she entered the Inhalatorium. They would not recover, in spite of

the faith with which, their nostrils dilated and eyes vacant, they breathed the life-giving gas. She thought of their slow gait, how they rested like lizards in the sun, and how they returned, prudently muffled up in shawls, at the first stroke of four. She, on the contrary, was able to bear the treacherous time when dampness is given forth by the water lacquered by twilight colors, when the firmament takes on the delicate shade of mauve, when the mountains stand out black against the background of the red or golden sky, when the sea is only a great mirror frosted with silver, and a single star sparkles in the west, like a little white diamond. Then her thoughts became tinged with melancholy; a reproach, or at least a regret, was mingled with her joy, although lightly and naturally, and it was only the shadow of a cloud. If others were suffering, she too had suffered. Why should she not have the right to a little happiness?

Nevertheless, at that precious moment, absorbed in herself, she was enjoying the sweet warmth, the light; everything seemed

good to her, pleasant and happy. She
found the faces about her more attractive,
the intonations of their voices sounded more
caressing in her ears. Raymond was walking behind her; she turned for a moment to
pick a hedge rose and met his eyes fixed on
her face, and they struck deep into her soul;
it gave her a shock, and the nervous con-
cussion prevented her from realizing for a
moment the material form of the vision, what
beautiful eyes the young man had, eyes of a
soft, but deep, blue, and all the manly youth-
fulness of his form, his native nobility. She
turned away quickly, ashamed, as though she
had been surprised in undress; but her sense
of shame did not take away from her satisfaction in feeling that she was there, and at
the same time feeling herself, and saying to
herself, that she was the same Minnie who
had come, in the beginning of the winter, so
delicate, so sad, and so discouraged, to this
country of rest and sunshine for invalids.
The same? No, most certainly quite another.
And yet.... She also felt amazement, which
was charming in its way, in looking for her-

self not to recognize herself, and when she recognized herself to find that she was no longer the same.

Singular uneasiness, exquisite pain were hers till the evening, when Raymond and Minnie felt, without knowing it, the love which was smouldering within them ; if they spoke to each other they blushed or turned away their faces, or else if they happened to look at each other they felt penetrated by a sweetness — a sweetness so sweet that they would have been glad to stop the flight of time and make the day last forever.

What did' they say? Nothing in particular. Did they try to draw near to each other? No, they were especially afraid of touching each other. However, they did not stay apart, for they were electrified by a reciprocal attraction ; but as soon as they had exchanged a few words it seemed to them as if everybody was looking at them, going to divine their hidden feelings ; then they would try to leave each other, but without success.

The breakfast was a diversion ; neither of them had any appetite, and yet, under the

thick, dark shade of an enormous, wide-
spreading pine-tree, the repast in the open
air, furnished by a little inn, was conducive
to merry faces, smiling and feasting, to the
lively play of white teeth and the pres-
tidigitation of forks. The saffron-colored
bouille-abaisse, the rainbow-hued fish caught
on the rocks, the red lobsters, and, still more,
the cordial understanding, the friendly conversation, all contributed to the joyful pleasure of eating their fill and drinking a drop
too much of white wine or sparkling Asti;
but Raymond and Minnie were neither
hungry nor thirsty, and the others noticed
it, but said nothing.

After they had sought the shade of the
pine woods, and had sat down on the dry,
short grass starred with Easter daisies, with
their backs to the hill and their eyes resting
on the sea, where the orange-colored sail of
a fishing-boat looked like the wing of a sea-
gull on the surface of the water, when the
young girls and boys had begun to play puss
in the corner, and Jean and Monsieur Ferrier were smoking and taking a walk, Ma-

dame Ferrier, with a motion of the head, pointed out Minnie and Raymond to her old friend.

Apart, standing near together without looking at each other, not touching each other, nor even speaking, they were looking straight before them at the sky and the sea.

" Don't you think," she said, in a low voice, " that they would make a well-matched couple ? "

Madame Rugles looked at her in amazement, and seeing that she smiled thought she was jesting.

" Are you in fun ? "

" They are not in fun, themselves," said Madame Ferrier. " Look at them ; you know much more extraordinary things have happened. Here they come towards us. How thoughtful they look ! Your Minnie looks as pretty as a pink."

" For heaven's sake, my dear," said Madame Rugles, very low and with eagerness, " think what you are saying."

" Well ! What harm is there in it ? "

"The harm, oh! Noémie, it would be too much happiness; you don't think..."

"Hush!" said Madame Ferrier; "here they come..."

They smiled at their children, who seriously, with strangely bright eyes, intense and moist, smiled back at them with that look of confused happiness which seems ready to laugh or burst into tears.

Bounding like a deer, Colette, who had disappeared, suddenly came towards them. She knelt down before the mammas with her hands full of pink and white blossoms.

"The almond-trees are in bloom," she said; "there is a whole field of them down there; pink ones and white ones, and they smell good, they smell delicious, they smell sweet! Smell of them, papa, and see!"

"They are very early," said Monsieur Ferrier; "who would believe, when the snow is falling in Paris, that here it is already April?"

"April," repeated his wife with a smile, while Colette, carrying the flowers to Minnie's and Raymond's faces, compelled them, too, to smell the lovely blossoms, hardly opened, exclaiming:

"April! April!"